## *Comments from Participants in Theatre of Life Workshops**

"**The Theatre of Life** works with body, mind, and spirit using the metaphor of theater. The natural order process is realized through the direct registry of frequency that leads to personal experience."
— *Lily Jean Haddad, Medina, OH*

"**The Theatre of Life** is an opportunity to develop tools to perceive and then embody the more of who you are."
— *Vera Isaac, Vernon, BC*

"**The Theatre of Life** is a life-changing, life-enlivening system designed to assist you in becoming an individualized, integrated being so you can function creatively and consciously."
— *Sandra Coyne, Aurora, OH*

"Other personal work I have done gave me facts and information about how to live, but **The Theatre of Life** gave me experience in bringing these ways of living into being. It brings the inner to the outer."
— *Martha Weatherell, San Benito, TX*

"It is a profound shift to move from 'I was created' to 'I am creating.' I experienced creativity for the first time."
— *Hollis Johnson, San Diego, CA*

"**The Theatre of Life** deepened my knowing of myself and my potential for being a passionate, deep, loving, serving human being who makes a difference on this planet."
— *Bette Myerson, Taos, NM*

"This truly is graduate work in self-exploration and self-finding."
— *Lyle Springer, Soquel, CA*

"This approach is filled with concrete, practical tools I can use daily to remind myself that I am Player and have choices about how I bring character into being."
— Joan Cudhea, San Diego, CA

"**The Theatre of Life** helped me to integrate knowing into character expression. I have become more powerful in my ability to express my feelings, and my actions are congruent with my inner intention. I have many more choices of ways to be."
— Suzanne Himmelwright, Belvedere, CA

"I have learned how urgent it is for me to live consciously and to be all I can be."
— Katharina Bruner, New York, NY

"As a result of this method, I have a new hope and expectancy of being the More I've always known was there but couldn't quite grab hold of."
— Rebecca Nerison, Seattle, WA

"**The Theatre of Life** requires a very high level of commitment and the willingness to experience what is necessary for growth in consciousness. The urge to grow must be present."
— Susan Guthrie, Chesterland, OH

"I kept digging in the garden of my inner being, pulling weeds, finding beautiful flowers, cultivating and planting qualities of being to replace the weeds. Patterns popped to the surface of my consciousness. Negativity, self-judgment, and lack of self-worth were tied tightly to resistance. In order to break the spider-web strands that had been so intricately woven in the far-distant past, the Work became a way of life, the process being the Work."
— Carol Adams, San Diego, CA

---

*\*Comments here, on the back cover, and throughout the text are excerpted from issues of* Emerging, *a publication of Teleos Institute. www.teleosinstitute.com*

# The Theatre of Life

## Other Books by Arleen Lorrance

The Love Principles

The Two

Images

India Through Eyes of Love

Born of Love

The Love Project Way
(with Diane Kennedy Pike)

Why Me? How to Heal What's Hurting You

Musings for Meditation

Buddha From Brooklyn

Channeling Love Energy
(with Diane Kennedy Pike)

The Love Project

# The Theatre of Life

*Exercising
Creative Jurisdiction
Over Self*

## Arleen Lorrance

*A Teleos Imprint Book*
LP Publications ~ Scottsdale, AZ

 *A Teleos Imprint Book*

Published by LP Publications
7119 E Shea Blvd.
Suite 109 PMB 418
Scottsdale, AZ 85254-6107

Copyright © 2011 by Arleen Lorrance

All rights reserved. This book, or parts thereof, may not be reproduced in any form without permission.

The Teleos Institute World Wide Web site address is
http://www.teleosinstitute.com

**Library of Congress Cataloguing-in-Publication Data**

Lorrance, Arleen, 1939-
   The theatre of life : exercising creative jurisdiction over self / Arleen Lorrance. -- 1st ed.
     p. cm.
 ISBN 978-0-916192-55-6 (alk. paper)
1. Self-actualization (Psychology) 2. Role Playing. I. Title.
BF637.S4L675 2011
158.1--dc23
                              2011019231

ISBN: 978-0-916192-55-6

First edition: June, 2011
Printed in the United States of America

*In tribute to*

*Irene Dailey*

*and*

*In gratitude to*

**Constantin Stanislavski**

## *Acknowledgements*

I am grateful to all the participants over the more than 26-year history of **The Theatre of Life** work. They pioneered along with me to help refine the program and they provided me with the great joy of being present as they consciously changed their lives to fulfill more of their potential.

I was profoundly blessed through all those creative years to have Diane Kennedy Pike (a.k.a. Mariamne Paulus) as my associate director. She provided the participants with valuable input, meaningful exercises, wonderful meditations, and superb critiques of their ongoing work. She was and is my most important support system and a master teacher.

A long line of influences contributed to the creation of **The Theatre of Life,** all of which enriched my creativity and enabled me to conceive of and then develop this comprehensive program.

I begin my list with radio, which served to provoke my imagination during my formative years and led to my reenacting all the shows after I listened to them.

When I was about ten, Herman Semel, the manager of the local movie theatre, started a Birthday Club for children to attend prior to the Saturday movie matinee. I began entertaining in the Club and by the time I was 11 I wrote, directed, costumed, and starred in plays performed right there in the theatre.

At age 12 my mother took me to singing and dramatic lessons with Charlie and Kasha Lowe in the CBS building in Manhattan. I also took tap dance with their nephew, Fred Bennett. Those were great times and I can still do a time step and a soft shoe.

Being accepted to the Drama Department of The High School of Performing Arts at age 13 was a major turning point in my life. I received excellent training in acting, speech, and dance. It was there that I first heard of Constantine Stanislavski and was exposed to some of his techniques. I am grateful to many of my teachers: Ruthel Provet, Marjorie Dycke, Bel Kaufman, Shirley Katz, Herbert Latner, and others who demanded excellence of me. I thrived on being called to my highest and best.

Following high school I had the privilege of studying on scholarship at the Herbert Berghof Studio with Irene Dailey and Uta Hagen, and at the New Dance Group with Anna Sokolow. Stanislavski's techniques were at the forefront of my studies.

Eighteen years as a professional allowed me to put into practice all that I had learned, but it was my spiritual teacher Evelyn Nolt who guided me to awakening to Cosmic Consciousness and to the eventual unfolding of **The Theatre of Life.**

◇◇◇◇◇◇◇◇◇◇◇◇◇

Special thanks to Dianne Grassé for her careful review of the text for this book. One of her special attributes is her thoroughness in everything she does.

Most especially I appreciate the editorial and production skills of Diane Kennedy Pike in the design and layout of this material. Diane is truly a creative artist who uses her many talents to enrich us all.

## Note to the Reader on the Origin and Evolution of *The Theatre of Life*

The material in this book grew out of the teachings of the Ancient Wisdom and the work of Constantin Stanislavski at the Moscow Art Theatre. It is based on the author's experiential work with these two predominant influences.

In the introduction to *Building A Character* by Stanislavski, theatre director Joshua Logan recalls a meeting with the master in 1931. Stanislavski told Logan he must not try to copy his work but rather "Let it make you think further." [page xv]

In an explanatory note in the same book, Elizabeth Reynolds Hapgood reports that Stanislavski's

> ...creative and artistic genius was never fully satisfied; it urged him on to the very day of his death to search for, to test, to choose new approaches to the art of acting, so that he hesitated to sum up any conclusions as final. He always hoped to find a better path to his high goal. Moreover he was fearful lest his written record might assume the aspect of ... rigid rules, a kind of bible. The thing that finally persuaded him to share his results by means of the printed word with artists throughout the world was the argument that others might receive some stimulus from them to strike out into new paths of their own. [page vii]

That is precisely what the creator of **The Theatre of Life** has done; she created a path of her own. Hapgood continued to say that Stanislavski called his system "...a whole way of life." Indeed! In this version of his teaching, ordinary folks are encouraged to consciously create their lives just as an actor creates a role for the stage.

# Contents

Introduction — i

**ACT ONE: Who Am I?** — 1

    Scene 1: *The Versatile Actor* — 3
    Scene 2: *Knowing Who You Really Are* — 8
    Scene 3: *Developing Your Talent* — 15
    Scene 4: *Creating Characters* — 25
    Scene 5: *The Disciplined Creative Artist* — 29
    Scene 6: *What Is Your Motivation?* — 36
    Scene 7: *Truthfulness* — 43

**ACT TWO: How Am I?** — 53
**Creating an Environment for Becoming**

    Scene 1: *Creating an Inner Environment for Becoming* — 55
    Scene 2: *Concentration* — 65
    Scene 3: *Expanding Concentration from the Inside Out* — 69
    Scene 4: *Conscious Reality Creation and Choice Making* — 74
    Scene 5: *How Am I?* — 77
    Scene 6: *A Sense of Truth* — 84
    Scene 7: *Units and Objectives* — 90

*Continued on next page*

## ACT THREE: What Am I?     111

| | | |
|---|---|---|
| Scene 1: | How Player Experiences Itself | 113 |
| Scene 2: | Feelings vs. Emotions | 116 |
| Scene 3: | Empowering Self Through Recall | 120 |
| Scene 4: | Enhancing Feeling Expression Through Outer Stimuli | 127 |
| Scene 5: | Living in the Now Moment | 132 |
| Scene 6: | Communion | 135 |
| Scene 7: | Sustaining Conscious Communion | 144 |
| Scene 8: | Communion with Self | 147 |
| Scene 9: | The Energy Involved in Self-Communion | 152 |
| Scene 10: | What Am I? How Do I Communicate with Myself? | 157 |
| Scene 11: | Oneness | 163 |

## ACT FOUR: Why Am I?     165

| | | |
|---|---|---|
| Scene 1: | Why Am I Here? | 167 |
| Scene 2: | Adapting | 170 |
| Scene 3: | The Life Story | 172 |
| Scene 4: | Motivating Forces | 175 |
| Scene 5: | Objectives | 181 |
| Scene 6: | Being Guided by the Unknown Super Objective | 186 |
| Scene 7: | The Unbroken Line | 188 |
| Scene 8: | How Our Lives Are Affected by Others | 191 |
| Scene 9: | Discovering the Character's Makeup | 193 |
| Scene 10: | The Inner Creative State | 195 |

*Continued on next page*

**ACT FIVE: On What Instrument
Do I Play Life's Music?**    203

| | | |
|---|---|---|
| Scene 1: | Knowing More About Your Instrument | 205 |
| Scene 2: | Patterns and Values | 208 |
| Scene 3: | Characters and Types | 212 |
| Scene 4: | Practicing Adaptation and Self-Expression | 217 |
| Scene 5: | Conscious Characterization | 220 |
| Scene 6: | Fluidity of Motion | 223 |
| Scene 7: | Restraint and Modulation | 227 |
| Scene 8: | Speech and Diction | 229 |
| Scene 9: | Intonations, Tempos, and Functioning Consciously | 233 |
| Scene 10: | Making an Imprint | 238 |
| Scene 11: | Subtext | 241 |
| Scene 12: | A Principled Approach to Theatre | 244 |
| Scene 13: | Patterns of Accomplishment | 248 |
| Scene 14: | The Natural Laws of Living | 251 |

**ACT SIX: I Am
Preparation for Creating
a Life Role**    253

| | | |
|---|---|---|
| Scene 1: | Preparation | 255 |

**Ways of Preparing:**

| | | |
|---|---|---|
| Scene 2: | Fresh Acquaintance | 261 |
| Scene 3: | Artistic Analysis | 265 |
| Scene 4: | External Circumstances | 267 |
| Scene 5: | Appraising the Facts | 271 |

*Concluded on next page*

## ACT SIX: I Am *(cont.)*
### Preparation for Creating a Life Role
**The Period of Creation:**
| | | |
|---|---|---|
| Scene 6: | Emotional Experience | 276 |
| Scene 7: | Creative Objectives | 282 |
| Scene 8: | The Super-Objective | 290 |
| Scene 9: | Physical Embodiment | 298 |
| Scene 10: | Physical Embodiment (cont.) | 302 |
| Scene 11: | Physical Embodiment (cont.) | 307 |
| Scene 12: | Physical Embodiment (cont.) | 311 |
| Scene 13: | Conscious Embodiment | 314 |
| Scene 14: | Direct Registry of Frequencies | 316 |

| | |
|---|---|
| Sources of Inspiration and Training for the Creation of **The Theatre of Life** | 319 |
| About the Author | 323 |

## *Introduction*

I remember reading about the CEO of a big company in Los Angeles who became stuck in traffic on the way to work one morning. He sat in his expensive Mercedes contemplating calling the office on his cellular phone when he began to have a serious change of heart. He looked from his creamy leather seats to his silk suit and gold cuff links, out through the tinted windows into the freeway turned parking lot. His mind took a literal flight of fancy as he pictured himself swinging on a hammock on a South Sea Island beach. What he did next sounds more fictional than real.

The CEO of the big company turned off his motor, left his car with the keys in it, walked on the shoulder to the next exit, and quit. He left his job, his security, his life as he had known it, and he created a whole new reality for himself on that envisioned South Sea Island. As far as I know, he is living there still, in the sun and the surf, happily ever after.

When I read this true story, I thought, "Hey, this would make a great scene in a movie." Who would ever believe that this could happen in real life?

It does happen. It happens every day to people

who wake up and make new choices. It happens to people who make "real life" whatever they want it to be. It happened to me!

The CEO was wealthy and could alter his life in an instant. I was not. His money helped with the decision-making, but the ability to radically change came because he did not identify himself with his role. It was as if he were an actor who had grown weary of being cast in the part of the successful businessman. He looked the part and carried it well, but that wasn't all that he was. He wanted a turn at playing a relaxed beach bum with few responsibilities. I, too, chose a new life just when the old one seemed to offer greater financial security through a promotion.

For over 18 years I lived as a professional actor, director, and drama coach, primarily in New York City. I also headed up the Speech and Theater Department in a Brooklyn high school. I felt rewarded in my work until, at the age of 29, I suffered heart disease caused by a virus. I had been a vital, highly energetic young woman. The pericarditis drained me of most of my life force. I dropped to 97 pounds and for six weeks had no strength to perform the simplest of bodily functions. The process of recovery took another six months.

The serious illness was the catalyst for a complete turnaround in my life. I came to see it as a spiritual awakening in which my heart center (heart chakra) was opened for the first time. This was followed by breakthroughs to Cosmic Consciousness, a knowing of the energy world, and experiencing my oneness with all that is. I was led to a study of wisdom teachings and, as a result, began to experience dissatisfaction with my life as an actor and with my living conditions in a concrete city whose frenetic tempo made it difficult to maintain inner stillness.

I became more interested in being of service to humanity than in being a working actor. My studies intensified and before long, I was taken to "classes" in my sleep where I was taught about the power of unconditional love. When I embodied that love and prevented a potentially violent fight at the high school where I worked, I was led to initiate **The Love Project.** Six simple Love Principles came to me on a ray of light as I sat in my office after the altercation:

> *Have no expectations, but rather abundant expectancy;*
> *Problems are opportunities;*
> *Create your own reality consciously;*
> *Provide others with opportunities to give;*
> *Be the change you want to see happen instead of trying to change anyone else; and*
> *Receive all people as beautiful exactly as they are.*

In a seven-month period, **The Love Project** turned the high school around from a place of despair to one in which learning, caring and love prevailed.

**The Love Project** was heralded in numerous newspaper stories, in scores of television interviews, in the magazine *Today's Education* and in a feature story prepared for *Look Magazine*. **The Love Principles** went on to be incorporated into everyday usage in the English language, in business, politics, and interpersonal relationships, as well as in New Thought teachings. As a result of my contribution, the Board of Education of the City of New York offered me a high paying job to start Love Projects throughout the school system.

I knew that Love Projects needed to begin as grass roots endeavors. A specialist could not bring radical change from the outside. Moreover, like the CEO caught in traffic, I felt caught in the harshness of city life. I longed to be surrounded by green. I wanted to know the west and the Pacific Ocean. I needed a complete change for the sake of my soul. Could my husband and I quit our jobs and simply drop our lives as we had known them? Could we leave our families and all our friends? Could we set out into the unknown with no real security? I was 31 years old; Dick was 54. The answer was yes.

After transporting our belongings and ourselves to San Diego, we had only $10,000 with which to start new lives. It was a courageous move and one that completely changed my life.

Things proceeded like a fast-paced movie script. Within three months I met Diane Kennedy Pike, best-selling author and widow of Episcopal Bishop James A. Pike. A year later she and I set out on an extraordinary work across the continent, teaching people ways to function more consciously and to express unconditional love. That work has persisted for 40 years and has touched the lives of many thousands of persons.

Had I never made the move from New York, I might never have had that profound opportunity.

Still, the world of theater remained alive in me. All my training seemed to be calling, demanding to be used. I knew I didn't want to return to New York, nor to the rat race of looking for acting jobs. I wanted something more. I began rereading the works of the great master Constantin Stanislavski, the founder of what is known as "Method Acting." I saw material there that I had completely missed in earlier readings. Stanislavski had studied yoga and spiritual principles. What I had failed to see before was that he was imparting these to his students at the Moscow Art Theater through his teaching of acting.

As I read, I also listened to what I considered erroneous language used by individuals who were doing consciousness work. They spoke of "having a higher self" which guided them to their best functioning. I saw that if we "had a higher self," we were identified with something lesser. I knew that each of us *is* the Higher Self.

Theater and consciousness work came together for me in that realization. If an actor were to become identified with the character he is playing, he would never be able to play any other type of role. But actors know better. They know themselves to be creative artists who bring characters into being for a short time and then return them to wardrobe.

I realized that Shakespeare was right, life is a stage and we are all Players. **The Theatre of Life** came into being in that moment. I saw that we "ordinary people" need to know that we are living on the stage of life. We are Players (Higher Selves) who bring characters into being. Alas, many of us choose to embody the same role our whole lives. We become the character we are playing because we don't understand that we can make choices. We don't know that each of us *is* the Higher Self that has been expressing itself through our familiar personality.

Having been an actor, I knew how wonderful it was to experience variety and to call forth a full range of qualities and characteristics. I could be anyone. I knew this was true for everyone. I envisioned a program that would teach others how to create their life roles more consciously. Since 1981, hundreds of participants have changed their lives for the better through work in **The Theatre of Life.** They have been liberated from bondage to a single sense of self and are now free to become whatever they wish in every moment.

Life is a stage, and we are all Players.
Life is a half-hour situation comedy, or a two-hour movie thriller, and we are the actors laughing our heads off or creating panic and fear. Knowing this can be very practical.

About fifteen years ago, I found myself in a very frightening situation. I was co-leading a Journey into Self (one of our foreign travel experiences) to India, Nepal, and Sri Lanka. At the end of the tour, as we

## Introduction vii

were departing from the Sri Lankan airport, four armed and ominous-looking military police grabbed me by my arms. They whisked me off to a private locked room for interrogation. I had no idea what I had done. Separated from my group, I could hardly breathe. My heart raced. The officers spoke rapidly to each other in a language I couldn't understand. I felt very small and vulnerable in their midst. Suddenly the door opened and an officious and highly-decorated officer entered, followed by three at-the-ready attaches. I didn't know if I should feel like a very important person or a potentially dead one.

This last thought was my saving grace. It pulled me from utter panic into remembering that I had a role in the reality that was being created here. There were more role options than "important person" or "corpse." I didn't know yet what they were, but I was able to remind myself that there was a full repertoire of characters from which I could choose.

Aware that I was definitely in "The Theatre of Life" at that moment, I began to observe myself in the interaction. I had made myself very frightened. This could be interpreted as trying to conceal something. I could not become aggressive or outraged, because that was not the role of women in that culture.

After the "arresting" officers had briefed the Chief Officer, an interpreter spoke to me. He explained that when I had entered the country I reported that I had x-number of US dollars on my person. Now, upon my exit, I was reporting 3 times that amount. They wanted to know where and how I got the money. The question was spoken brusquely and with an accusing finger. All eyes were on me.

Remembering the discrepancy, I relaxed and chose to embody the character of a composed, responsible, and sincere visitor from the United States. I announced to the officers that I had reported my personal funds on entering and had forgotten to list the group tipping fund that I was also carrying. I smiled at them, thinking I would be out the door in the next minute.

The officers looked grim. Once again, they all began talking. When they looked back at me, their eyes narrowed, their mouths pulled taut, and their shoulders hunched, I stopped breathing and I wondered what a Sri Lankan prison was like. They had my passport and my plane tickets. I was completely isolated. They could have forced the rest of my group onto the plane at gunpoint if necessary. This was no laughing matter.

I took a quick breath, trying to evaluate the situation. I had been honest with them, but that had not worked. I had done nothing wrong, but that did not matter. I remembered an earlier trip to the Middle East when one of the young men in our group was taken away because drugs were found on his person. He was imprisoned and not heard from again.

I needed to calm myself. In order to choose how I was going to play this scene, I needed to be centered and clear. I looked around at the setting and the officers. As I took a deep breath, I began to see all of them as actors! Their costumes were perfect and their demeanor gave just the right tone to inspire immobilizing fear in the tourist. They raised their voices at all the right moments. Their lines were delivered right on cue. And, they used carefully rehearsed gestures for impact. Seeing them in this light, I was more impressed by their performances than I was frightened by what was actually taking place. I looked for an opening.

Gruffly, the Chief Officer wanted to know what purchases I had made. Suddenly I saw a chance for my release.

In the few seconds I had to respond, I began to create a different character from the one I had been playing. I chose "dumb tourist." I knew this would appeal to them. I fleshed it out a little more by playing, "dumb female American tourist." I became wide-eyed. I reached into my travel bag and pulled out a handful of garnets that I had purchased. I had the receipt. I started to imagine that I was in the presence of officials who needed to be affirmed in their roles as "those in charge." I cast myself as the naive visitor who was so stupid that any fast-talking salesman in the streets of Sri Lanka could deceive her.

I pulled my face into a serious expression that indicated I needed their help. They softened. I held the garnets in my hand and let my mouth fall open. They began leaning forward in their importance, ready to make a judgment about the purchase. "They're real aren't they?" I asked, with the fullest innocence I could muster.

The officers all leaned over, peering into my small, cupped hand. They deferred in their response to the Chief, while I continued to play this new role of "dumb female American tourist." I was, in my silence, beseeching them to tell me I had made a wise purchase, simultaneously communicating, "Don't you see, I'm not the type to pull a fast one by taking money out of your country illegally."

The Chief threw his head back laughing. They all began talking and laughing. I had either been taken or I had paid too much. Anyone that stupid wasn't smart enough to smuggle money out of the country.

My face communicated my chagrin as I continued to play my role. How could I have been so dumb? I felt a little bolder. I begged the Chief, through the interpreter, to tell me it wasn't so, that I hadn't made a bad purchase. This caused him to laugh even more. He waved his hand at me and toward the door. The "arresting officers" quickly removed me from the interrogation room and returned me to my group.

I had been caught in a potentially horrendous "real life" situation. I had been saved because I had the savvy to view this scene as taking place in a theatre of life where I could choose who I would be and how I would respond.

When we think of ourselves as Players creating roles, we know we can change them whenever we wish. Chuck the costume and makeup and go to wardrobe to find something that suits us better in this moment. Create new dialogue. Play in a scene that is much more exciting and stimulating than what we had previously settled into and called "real life."

Mary Tyler Moore, a fine actress who handles

## Introduction    xi

drama and comedy equally well, left a starring role in her own television series, New York News, because the character and story line didn't have enough depth for her. How many of us have the courage to quit a good paying job, a leading role, because it lacks depth and meaning? How many of us could leave a long-standing life role because it seems to be going nowhere?

We can do it if we know we are not the job we are holding or the role we are playing. We can do it if we know we are Players who can say "no" to what is not challenging, even if it's successful. We are Players who can courageously say "yes" to the untried, the daring, the risky, the creatively stimulating.

I invite you to expand your definition of real life to include the understanding that you are a participant in **The Theatre of Life.** You are Player, the actor, the director, the writer, the agent, the designer, the stage manager, the producer, and often even the audience, in your own life production. The only thing that is truly real is what you decide is real, and you have the power to alter that reality, scene by changing scene.

Join me up here on the stage as we pursue an adventure of liberation in which you can have the starring role.

In **The Theatre of Life** you will discover who you really are, and, as a result, how powerful you can be. You will learn the importance of creating a nourishing environment, both in your outer world and in your inner self.

In **The Theatre of Life,** you'll be surprised to learn that no one ever "has" feelings. Instead, you, Player, choose, create, shape, and express the feelings you awaken in yourself.

You will identify your life purpose and the importance of having objectives to guide you through each day.

You will gain new strength in relationships through adapting to others rather than accommodating them.

Professional actors are able to play a multitude of roles because they are creative, flexible, adept in body and vocal instrument, and highly disciplined. You can do the same.

If you have been appearing in a dull and dated play, you can end the long run and consciously take yourself into rehearsal for a new opening night.

The potential lies in you to bring a whole new person into being. Actors do it every time they step out on the stage. And so can you. If you have been waiting endlessly for someone else to cast you in a new role, the wait is over. You, as casting director, have determined that you are perfect for the new part. As you develop the skills necessary to become the creative artist of your own life, the rest will unfold with pleasure and wisdom in **The Theatre of Life.**

With this in mind I have written the text in a way that will allow you to engage actively with the material so that you can do the exercises, try out the concepts in daily life, and actively journal about insights, observations and discoveries.

# The Theatre of Life

*Exercising
Creative Jurisdiction
Over Self*

# ACT ONE

# Who Am I?

# 2     *The Theatre of Life*

"The key factor in being conscious is to have a purpose. When we are without purpose we are drawn outside ourselves, as if magnetically, to what others think or want from us."
— *Carol Adams, San Diego, CA*

"I used to make logical choices but suffer emotionally. I had trouble staying in the moment. I discovered that when I focused on being fully present that relieved anxiety, fear, and the desire to be someplace else."
— *Tom McCarthy, Del Mar, CA*

"I discovered the places where I am attached, through affection and distaste, to character patterns; beloved patterns such as feeling harried/out of time got shifted easily through conscious embodiment and new facial expressions."
— *Suzanna Neal, San Diego, CA*

"I observe that I am in want and have fear and expectations only when my character thinks it is in charge. When Player is directing, I feel incredible power, power to move obstacles that have prevented me from being who I know I am."
— *Mary Ann McCarthy, San Francisco, CA*

"I don't have to hold back any longer. I can go into a situation with the power of a purpose and feel strong and focused. I see my work as freeing myself from old patterns and opening to the more of creativity."
— *Diana Farquharson, Belleville, ON*

"I never thought in terms of purposes, objectives, and activities before, so my life seemed to have little meaning. Now I see how having them gives meaning to my remaining years. I want to be as alive in my 'real' life as I have felt in Act One."
— *Esther Bell, Ashland, OR*

"I discovered there are patterns not in conscious alignment with my main purpose. I now know that these patterns can be released, altered or brought into alignment with purpose by examining, clarifying, practicing, watching, and being willing to stay focused."
— *Eleanor Arnau, San Diego, CA*

## Scene One
## *The Versatile Actor*

There are many actors who are always the same when you see them in a movie. It seems as if they are playing the same role in every film. To say that they are "playing" the same role may give them too much credit. More likely, these actors are simply being "themselves," repeatedly, no matter what costumes they are wearing.

If they are dull actors, you tire of them quickly. When you have seen one of their performances, you have seen them all. If, on the other hand, they are handsome, sexy, mysterious, delightful, or unusual, few of us care if they bring themselves to the screen again and again. Millions of people enjoy Nicolas Cage films. He mostly plays Nicolas Cage, but he is loved for his intensity and uniqueness. No one cares if he always sounds the same. People want him to sound that way. That is how they know and love him. He is the "good guy" screen hero.

The same is true of women screen counterparts. Julia Roberts is the girl next door, or the one you wished lived next door. She has freshness, lots of energy, and an open face. You can always count on her being Julia Roberts and you want her to be Julia Roberts, maybe because you aren't! If she maintains this desirable image, you can at least have it through her.

Cage and Roberts have that special something that is present whenever you go to see their films. They are who they are and you pay your money to keep them that way on the big screen.

Many of us live our lives this way. We become single role actors. We unconsciously developed a personality and we go on being it, no matter what the circumstances or with whom we engage. We say, "This is who I am." We are not "playing" this role. We *are* this role. If who we happen to be is pleasant, our friends and family delight that we go on being it. If who we are is irritating, not many people in our acquaintance enjoy attending our performances. Our theaters remain relatively empty. Popularity is measured by how many people we draw to us.

There are other actors who rarely play the same role twice. Some of them do such interesting things on the screen that it takes you a long time into the movie before you even recognize them. Then, suddenly, you say, "Hey, that's Lawrence Olivier!" or, "That's Meryl Streep." You watch Tom Hanks go from the character he created for *Big* and wonder how on earth he brought Forest Gump or the sergeant in *Saving Private Ryan* into being. Tom Hanks is not just an actor; he is an artist.

You too can be an artist in **The Theatre of Life.** You can become whomever you choose. You don't have to go on playing the same set of personality characteristics. You can add a little adventure to your life and become something different, some-

## Act One: Who Am I?

thing unexpected. You can always be at the ready to have your outer personality match what you experience within yourself.

This may not be as radical as it sounds. You have probably done this several times in your life and simply not thought of it this way. For example, your teenager breaks curfew and you wait at home, pacing the floor in the middle of the night. You mutter a few choice words. You try to decide if you will pounce when you hear the key in the lock. But during these moments of preparing yourself, you remember your teen years and you decide not to be too ferocious. You begin to practice just how much firmness and disappointment you will express. You move your body into an appropriate shape. You lower your voice to catch the ominous quality of your message. You begin to gesture as you practice your delivery. When your teenager enters the house, you are ready, fully rehearsed. Your child sees a side of you not previously played on the stage at home. You are very convincing and the teen goes to bed filled with chagrin. You, then, release the performance, chuckle to yourself in your satisfaction, and retire for the night, returning to your usual gait and personality.

You have just played a role, one very different from how you usually portray yourself. You brought into being the qualities and demeanor necessary to communicate your point. You did this by exercising your will and aligning with the creative part of yourself that can bring anything into being. You became Player and you put on the costume of outraged parent.

In order to play different roles, you must first know that you are *not* the long-running role you seem always to be playing. You need to know who you truly are.

## *Exercise:*

Observe yourself in conversation with friends. As you speak with them, identify (for yourself, without calling attention to what you are doing) habits or quirks you employ while you speak. It may be that you talk with your hands waving, or you tense up when speaking or listening, or you avert your eyes or close them when speaking, or that you race through your words.

As you observe yourself doing any of the above, practice doing each habit or quirk consciously. Once you begin to consciously create the behavior, you will begin to strengthen your choice-making ability in relation to the behavior. For example, if your hands are always flying when you talk and you begin to make choices about doing that (when and how much), you will become more discriminating in your gestures and they, in turn, will add meaning to what you are saying rather than aimlessly flailing about.

## *Questions to Ask Yourself:*

At the end of each day during Act One you might ask yourself, "What is the most important thing I learned today?" and, "How could I have acted more

## Act One: Who Am I? 7

consciously?" The first question allows you to note and therefore to retain a growth step. The second prods you to examine behavior you observed and to make new choices where appropriate.

## Scene Two
## *Knowing Who You Really Are*

Who are you? Do you know?

Before you say, "This is a silly question. Of course I know who I am," listen to the answer you are giving. Are you identifying yourself by name, by role, by function, by sex? Are you speaking of your personality type? None of these is who you are.

When I first discovered this, I found it very disconcerting. I was, I thought, Arleen: a teacher, a wife, a good person, and a professional performer. I was creative, sensitive, and intelligent.

I was a list. I identified with my personality expression. I saw myself as others saw me, or, at least as I hoped they did.

But if I was not all I thought I was, who was I?

In the world of theater, actors know they create characters. They are not the roles they play. Rather, they are Players who create the characters. They don the characters' costumes, makeup, body shapes, movements, and attitudes, and give them life on the stage. At the end of the performance, the actors cleanse the characters from their faces with makeup remover, and hang the characters' clothing back in wardrobe.

## Act One: Who Am I?

Within a lifetime, you, as a human being, do the same thing. You create a character through which to function in the world. You choose the play (the family of characters) and the setting (the location and environment) in which to be born and to live out your life roles. When you finish with this life, you hang your character up and play it no more. The memory of your performance lingers in the hearts and minds of your relatives, friends, and colleagues, but the role itself has been taken out of the repertoire.

Who is this you who creates, embodies and finishes? Who are you? You are the power-to-be-conscious that brings the character, known by your name, into being every day. You are Player, strutting and gesturing on the stage of life through the form of a character.

Knowing this can transform your life. Once you know who you are in reality, you are never again a victim of circumstance. You no longer identify with an image of yourself. You no longer limit yourself to the illusion that you are a body, feelings, thoughts, skills, habits, or preferences. You discover that you are the one who chooses your preferences, nurses your habits, hones your skills, structures your thoughts, creates your feelings, and sustains the configuration known as your body.

Who are you? You are not your character (personality). You are not the roles you play in life. You are not your body, or your feelings, or your thoughts. You are not a small self in search of a Higher Self. Instead, you are that Higher Self.

You are creative consciousness. Like the actor on the stage, you develop the character through which you express, and you choose the roles you take on. You are Player who determines to a large degree the health of your body, and when you are conscious enough, its shape and how it looks. You are Player who becomes aware of energy in and through your solar plexus and then decides what feelings you will create. You are Player who is in charge of what your mind thinks and how those thoughts affect you. You are the conscious being that has creative jurisdiction over all your experiences and all that you bring into being.

When you know who you are, you leave *why* questions about yourself behind. You no longer berate yourself wondering, "*Why* did I do that?" or "*Why* didn't I act more in keeping with what is expected of me?" Asking *why* doesn't lead you to new behavior. Wondering *why* you are the way you are doesn't help you to become who you want to be or or go very far toward creating the new. Asking *why* is a way of remaining one step removed from self and one step behind the circumstance at hand. Knowing *why* something happened doesn't change anything, nor does it help you to cope with the events you are facing.

What does help is focusing on *who*. You might ask yourself, "*Who* am I in this moment and *what* do I need to do to change this unsatisfying reality?" When you focus on *who* you are, you function creatively.

When you begin to know yourself in this way, you accept responsibility for your life and your

## Act One: Who Am I?   11

choices. You no longer blame your parents or your early experiences for the problems or limitations from which you suffer today. Instead, your focus is on what you need to do for yourself today to become the more you wish to be.

Over the years I have worked with numerous people who remained wounded by instances of physical or sexual abuse in their childhood. Clinging to their memories and continuing to suffer them, these individuals were abusing themselves. They were battering themselves with memories and diminishing their self-images by dwelling on who they were then, instead of on who they could be now.

Many of these wounded people developed conditions in response to their early trauma. Some became obese. Others could not function in relationship. Still others suffered from low self-esteem, if not a psychological disorder. Many of these people were in therapy for years. There, they worked through the pain of the childhood imprint and reached a greater understanding of their condition. Concurrently, they attended workshops and self-help programs that fortified them and readied them for the next steps they needed to take toward alignment of the whole self. At that point, they were ready to do consciousness work, to create new realities about themselves and even about what had happened to them. They were ready to examine the spiritual dimensions of their situations, to forgive, to reclaim their power, and to turn their attention to who they were in that present moment.

When we identify with the character self who suffered the early assaults, we sometimes experience loss, as if something was taken from us. But when we come to know that we are not the character who suffered, we realize that nothing was ever lost. As Players, we have access to all that ever was, is now, or will be. We can reclaim what characters think is lost. For example, the safety we felt we lost due to a childhood trauma could be reclaimed as an adult by embracing safety as a quality we value and choose to embody. The past was just that — the past!

When we identify with the character from the past and feel unsafe, we are often immobilized. Internal voices issue threatening proclamations and we retreat deeper into self. To ease our stress, we might ask, "Why do I feel unsafe right now?" But "Why" questions produce mental responses to deal with feeling states. The feelings remain unchanged. The sense of danger persists.

When we move from identification with character to knowing self as Player, we can remind ourselves that feeling unsafe belongs to a character we used to embody at an earlier time in our lives. We can remind ourselves that we are no longer that character from the past. We can bring ourselves fully into the present moment and begin to ask "what" and "how" questions, rather than "why." Helpful questions might be, "*What* can I do to create a sense of safety? *How* can I change this reality? *What* do I need? *How* can I go forward with confidence?" "What" and "How" move us into action. "Why" moves us only into our heads.

Who are you? You are Player in whom limitless

## Act One: Who Am I? 13

potential resides. Through the character you create, you can bring almost anything into being. An affirmation that helps to remind us of who we really are: I am not character; I am Player who brings this character into being.

## *Exercise:*

Take time to do a study of your character/self from several points of view as listed below. In each case choose what is relevant to your early life, your formative years through age 12. Make notes under each item.

- **The time period** in which your character came into being
- **The country and location in the country**
- **The living conditions**
- **Specific values held by the family**
- **Ways of living** (customs and traditions)
- **Financial standing**
- **External appearance as a child** (how others described you and how you thought of yourself)
- **Predominant personality expressions as a child**

What specifics from your character's background still affect your character today?

Assess if there are any "specifics" (qualities, expressions, or ways of thinking) that no longer serve you even though they are still affecting you. Let go of what no longer serves you and watch to see if it crops up in the future so that you can consciously change it.

Looking over the whole of what influenced you early on in your life and what still remains alive for you, see if you can identify the overall essence that predominates in your character. It might be that you were born in dire times and grew up in cramped quarters. The predominant family values revolved around survival. You didn't have enough as a child and felt deprived and therefore you were very shy. Today, although you might be solvent, you might be frugal, careful, and remain shy. Your essence would be quiet and somewhat withdrawn. This, of course, is but one example. See what is true for you as you review your character study.

Once you identify your essence, embody it consciously when you are next in the presence of others. Observe yourself as you are creating it. Now, that essence is not simply overtaking your personality. Instead, you are making it a reality.

Observe others in your acquaintance to see if you can identify their essence. If it is different from yours, try it on for an hour. See how your personality changes under a different influence. If you like what you see, keep what feels good to you and watch how you can begin to change how you present yourself in the world. Continue to try on different essences.

## Scene Three
## *Developing Your Talent*

Very few actors become overnight successes. Most have been around for quite a while, having taken years of training in voice, speech, dance, fencing, acting technique, and scene study. When they are hired, in big parts or small, they draw on their training to help them create the role at hand. The director expects it of them. No one wants to train actors in their craft in the middle of rehearsing a production. There are skills actors must have and must be able to apply in all circumstances. Many of these same skills are essential for us as life-actors. Two of these skills are observing and directing.

An actor must be observant. What is going on in the scene around him? What is being asked of her as a character? What are the other characters doing and how does that affect him? What response does the behavior of others call forth from her? The actor has specific lines to say and actions given him by the playwright and the director. Yet, each time the actor speaks and moves it is as if it is happening for the very first time. By observing, the actor gives the audience the feeling that she is just now discovering what is taking place.

Following the observation, the actor then begins to direct his energy into the lines and actions.

**To create is to direct energy.** You choose a purpose, and focus on making it a reality. Your intention and your focus direct your energy. In establishing this unbroken creative line, your own initiative and follow-through carry you toward fruition. By directing your energy in an outward motion, you create from an inner source, aligning with all that is larger than you.

When an actor does this, you, in the audience, are convinced that the character the actor is playing has just chosen what to say and do. You follow closely because there is a sense of immediacy in what is taking place. The circumstance excites you and you wait for the next surprising line or the next laugh.

"Real" life is supposed to be spontaneous. But often, real life is repetitious and dull because you, as Player, are not fully present in the moment. You do not observe yourself and the choices you make of what to say and do. You do not direct your energies and therefore consciously contribute to how the life-scene will unfold. Instead, you repeat old performances you have given in similar circumstances. You are very predictable and, not surprisingly, the scene plays out as it has hundreds of times before. Then you wonder why nothing ever changes.

Let's cast you in a scene with a friend. She tells you she wants more attention from you and if she doesn't get it, she plans to leave the relationship. You are resistant and upset. While you want the re-

## Act One: Who Am I?   17

lationship to continue, you don't want to devote any more time to her needs than you already have. You look for ways to say this, but so many feelings come up at once that you feel choked. You are unwilling to expose your inner process and make yourself vulnerable in her presence. You are at a stalemate as she goes on with her demands. On the stage of life, this is a very dramatic scene.

If, at this point, you function unconsciously, the familiar patterns of behavior, already built into your character through years of practice, will automatically take over. You will react in easily recognizable ways. You might pout, stop speaking, withdraw into self, and stew. You might refuse to engage any further. Before long, when you are alone, anger will rise in you. Following some muttering, you might explode with epithets or volleys of blame. It is only at this point that you might wake up to realize that you have repeated non-productive behavior. You will then need to trace backwards to see how you fell into this trap.

In order to do the tracing or even to realize you behaved in this way, you need to be conscious and you must observe. This may sound simple, but not if you think of all the times you have gone on automatic and acted predictably and unsatisfactorily.

Every time you need to go backwards to trace the origins of your current difficulties you rob yourself of life-time that could be spent in moving forward to transformation.

In the scene with your friend, had you been conscious at the beginning of the exchange, you might have been observant. Then you would have noticed that you were beginning to congest your energy, to tighten, to pull back, and to resist. At that very moment, you could have begun to direct your responses and given yourself specific instructions about how to move your energy. You would have reminded yourself to breathe deeply, and to continue to do so. You would have directed yourself to listen to your friend as if for the first time, hearing her words and not your interpretation of them. You would have paid attention to the feeling energy being awakened in you and have made choices about what to feel. Then, you would have chosen the words you wanted to speak and the actions you wanted to take.

You would have continued to observe the impact on both your friend and yourself of the choices that you were making. Each observation would have enabled you to make a new and more appropriate choice. You would have directed yourself to complete the scene with her so that no energy remained to be expended at a later time. So often, when you are not functioning consciously, you hide, even from yourself, what is transpiring within you. Then you hear yourself complaining about the friend to others whom you deem sympathetic to your position.

To know self as Player in the midst of a lifescene is to know that you can be conscious in every moment. To be conscious is to continually observe your actions and to direct your unfolding choices.

When you truly know that in each moment you create the character through which you function in the world, you also open yourself to the potential for creating any characteristic, skill, and talent you wish. All too often you hear yourself say, "I can't play a musical instrument." You say that you don't have the talent for it, or can't learn it. The true obstacle is within self. You have separated yourself from the possibility. Characteristics, talents, qualities, and skills are universally available. When you know each of us is Player who creates the character, you can pick and choose the attributes you want to embody.

For years I could not fathom the sphere of music. Then I made up my mind (an interesting phrase meaning "I constructed a mental picture in which to believe") that I would open this world to myself. I took piano lessons and began to develop the physical skills necessary to serve my quest. As I progressed, albeit slowly, I noted and confronted a critical inner mental voice that persisted in delivering a negative message I had previously created. The voice said, "You can't do this."

After several months of practice and persistence, I began to create a new dialog within myself. As Player, I reminded the character, through whom I was having difficulty, that the talent associated with playing the piano was part of the human pool of consciousness. As a human, I could partake of this talent as a natural birthright.

During one of my lessons, a breakthrough occurred. It was as if a window opened, or a veil parted. Whatever separated my character from embodying this human talent fell away. Suddenly, I could "see" music. I could understand its principles. I had stepped into its world. During that half-hour,

I began to transpose what I was playing as if I had done that quite naturally all of my life. It was such a revelatory experience that my understanding of creativity itself began to expand.

I saw how most of us limit ourselves to mediocrity. We identify with ourselves as specific characters rather than knowing ourselves as Player who is capable of creating all things.

Whenever you say, "I can't," you are really describing the limitations you as Player have created for the specific role you are playing. The limitations are attributes of the character, not of Player-Self. You confirm those self-imposed limitations by proving that you are unable to do what you said you couldn't do. For example, "I can't write poetry." While you direct your energy into "I can't," you will never know if you can.

If you come to know yourself as Player, you can turn your focus away from your past character's history of not being able to write poetry and center yourself in the consciousness of the present moment of creating a new character. In this present moment, everything is possible. You can move from your literal view that saw the mountain peaks as high and beautiful, to allowing yourself to touch the feelings evoked by the peaks. Now you can relate that "a majestic range rose from where my feet ended, drawing the whole of my senses and my very breath to the jagged top." Already, you have begun to express yourself poetically. Not because you are newly able, but because you stepped out of your own way and allowed a capacity that had always been there to have life.

## Act One: Who Am I?

The Self can create every characteristic there is when it knows itself as Player. The same is true of skills and talents. We all have the capacity to make beautiful music, to be athletes, to paint, to draw, to run a business, to be a senator, to . . . anything. The question is whether we choose the characteristics to create the reality. When we know ourselves to be Player, we know that we have unlimited choices.

During my theatrical career, I surprised myself numerous times with my ability to play characters very different from how I thought of myself. It was always easy for me to play strong women or funny uninhibited types. But when, at age 28, I successfully played a craggy, aging, alcoholic prostitute, I was shocked at how convincing I was with qualities that were nothing like my usual personality. My husband said that he hardly recognized the woman on the stage. I was equally amazed, earlier in my career, that I was able to portray Shakespeare's Juliet with sweetness, softness and vulnerability. I never would have thought I could achieve that.

Our problem is that we try to talk ourselves out of possibilities before we ever give ourselves a chance. If we stop convincing ourselves of our limitations, we will discover what wonders emerge.

### *Exercise:*

To experience this for yourself, choose a simple physical activity that you know you can't perform. It could be touching your toes with both hands while keeping your knees straight or linking your arms from top to bottom behind your back. Try the feat to be sure you still can't do it. Then consciously begin the process of guiding yourself past your own limitations.

Invite a friend to help you with this experiment. Close your eyes and breathe deeply. Know yourself as Player and observe your character as a form that is here to fulfill your directions. Standing in a position of readiness, breathing and concentrating on your purpose, turn yourself away from any focus on identification with past character history. At a random moment, have your friend shout the command, "Do it!" At that moment, without thought, immediately do the task you "can't" do.

In most cases, you will join the ranks of hundreds before you and bypass your limited view of what you can do and proceed to perform a feat you believe you are incapable of performing.

If you were indeed able to perform the task, note that it was less the result of developing a new body skill and more a matter of staying out of the way. You tapped the pool of human capacity. You, as Player, were able to direct character to embody a larger will.

If you were only partially successful, or if you failed, continue to practice when you are alone, by saying "do it" at odd times. Do not focus on the task itself but rather on yourself as Player, who can create anything.

While there are many forms of learning, among the best are those which encourage you to embody rather than mentally process. To study through the mind is a logical and reflective endeavor in which you think about information. This is very different from kinesthetic learning in which you sense and feel and therefore come to know the material. I have given you information about the difference between Player and Character so that you can have a conceptual grasp of the two. Now I would encourage you to do a physical experience which will allow you to learn the distinction through your body so that you have an actual imprint on your consciousness.

## *The Zoo Experience:*

Write a descriptive paragraph about yourself as character and another about yourself as Player. In each case note applicable qualities, tempo-rhythm, prevalent behavior, etc. Review these before taking a trip to the zoo.

Your task at the zoo is to observe all the animals and find one that clearly speaks to you of yourself as character and another that speaks to you of yourself as Player. Don't choose birds, snakes, or water animals.

Once you select the two animals, spend two separate 20-minute segments in front of each animal enclosure studying and practicing embodying the animal: its movements, its sounds, and its tempo-rhythm. This will also give you an opportunity to practice focusing on a task without allowing distractions from outside yourself.

Then go home and practice embodying the two animals, all the while focusing on all the differences you notice between the animals and between yourself as character and yourself as Player. Make notes of what you discover.

Next, assume the position of the animal halfway so that you are half animal and half human. Practice simple household tasks observing once again the differences you notice between the two.

Then, maintaining the essence of the animals in your consciousness, move as your own character and then as Player.

As you proceed you will notice that you have greater awareness of yourself as character and as Player because you have given each a slightly different expression through the animals you chose.

**The purpose of the above experience is to allow you to feel the difference between character and Player in yourself so that you can begin to direct your life with more consciousness.**

This exercise might be more fun if you can get a friend to do the whole process with you, focused on his or her own character and Player self.

## Scene Four
## *Creating Characters*

Are you tired of seeing your same old face in the mirror every morning? Do you wish you looked like someone else? Wake up! Stop identifying with the face you are creating.

It is said that acting is make believe. It is indeed. Actors make themselves and others believe that what they are seeing is true. This is not only a definition of acting; it is a definition of life. You make believe that what you see is true. For example, you believe that the "costume" you are wearing is who you actually are. You believe that you are your personal history and that you cannot break from it. You make believe that you are limited to who you think you are, and then you are limited! You have given a believable performance of yourself. You yourself believe it, and others believe it all, too.

You become typecast as yourself.

The art form of acting is really doing, not pretending. If you want to be as glamorous as Angela Bassett or as nimble as Jackie Chan, it is not for you to imitate them. Instead, you must choose characteristics you see in them and embody them yourself. Rosie Perez is perky. What do you need to add to your personality to project the same kind of spunk? Will Smith is cool. How can you reduce stress in yourself so that you too can know that smoothness?

When you come to know that you are creating your character in each moment, you then have the capability to create any and all characteristics at any time.

Consider the quality "unworthy." You might say you are unworthy. What this really means is that you are choosing to play "unworthy," to identify with "unworthy," to repeatedly and unconsciously create "unworthy," to faithfully perform all the behavior associated with "unworthy."

Is it possible to change? Of course it is, but how? Well, you could attend workshops that focus on being deserving or self-affirming. Or you could do personal work on self to discover how you "got" the way you are, or "why" you are this way, and then begin to release the influencing past.

In the past, I have facilitated both of these approaches. The limitation of these methods is that you remain identified with the quality, or seek to replace it with another quality with which you will also identify. You see yourself as a set of particular characteristics. A set of particular characteristics cannot change itself.

Player can change any characteristic because he or she is not identified with any of them. The most wonderful difference between functioning as Player rather than character is that Player has the ability to change characteristics in an instant. Characteristics and qualities belong to character; action belongs to Player. No laborious process is necessary, only choice.

To create means to bring something into being as a result of directing energy. The energy does not belong to you, and neither does the creation. But the process of directing the energy is yours to do. You observe the change you want to see happen and you direct yourself to create the reality consciously. Creating characteristics is an act of directing energy in a specific outward motion. The result is tangible, yet impermanent. In every moment you are free creatively to make a new choice. You know yourself as creator rather than as the creation.

To know that you have the power to create something new, you must acknowledge that you have created what is already in place. It didn't just happen. If your character is judgmental, it is not because you were born that way. You chose it as a way of functioning. You directed your life energy into sustaining it. You say you wish to change it, but you imprison yourself with the view that this is simply the way you are.

## *Exercise:*

Practice breaking this cycle. Think of it as rehearsal time. Actors are constantly working at home, learning their lines and developing their characters. They select characteristics to bring to life. Then, they speak and act through them. Actors are able to determine if the characteristics are appropriate because they have embodied those characteristics and now know how they feel. Because they have given them full life, they can easily discard them because they have no attachment to characteristics that don't serve the role they are creating.

You can do the same thing with any characteristic you want to change. Take for example the characteristic of being judgmental. Here you are, Player, in the privacy of your own room. You don't need to inflict this practice session on anyone else. Alone and ready to emote, take a deep breath and make the choice to play "judgmental."

Think of the person about whom you are feeling judgmental. Stand up in the fullness of yourself and let your voice boom as if you were an evangelist. Choose your words so that they are particularly condemnatory. Be forceful and observe how much energy you are calling up for the task. Feel how hot your face gets and how tense you are making your body. Play it to the hilt so that you can experience how you create the characteristic "judgmental."

You might be shocked by how it feels to do this consciously. But once you have done it, it will be much harder for you to ever again do it unconsciously. In addition, once you have directed your energy in this way, you will know deep within yourself that you have equal power to create something other than this. As you created "judgmental," so too, and just as effectively, you can create unconditional receptivity, or any other quality you choose.

## Scene Five
## *The Disciplined Creative Artist*

In order to begin to know yourself as Player, who can bring any self-expression into being, it is helpful to develop disciplines by which to live. Did you bristle at the word discipline? Did you think of it as a restriction, or even a punishment? If you did, then you have a wonderful discovery ahead of you.

Disciplines are the banks of the river of our lives through which our creative life force can flow unimpeded. Disciplines help us to hold fast to our commitments. They enable us to stay on track and to function at our highest and best capacity. When we establish disciplines in our lives, we set the stage for our continued development of consciousness. Without them, we tend to function haphazardly and our creative energy spills out in all directions.

Anyone in the arts knows the importance of disciplines. The writer must write every day, even if it is just a page or two. If the dancer doesn't put in several hours of stretching and limbering up each day, the body cannot be as responsive as it needs to be. The painter is constantly practicing with techniques and improving upon them. The singer vocalizes every day, whether she will be performing or not.

When I was a child, I noted a difference between many of the other kids in the neighborhood and myself. When they would go out into the street to have a game of catch, they would throw the ball for a while, enjoy themselves, and then move on to another activity. There was little purpose to the game; they were simply playing.

When I asked a friend to play catch with me, I gave myself disciplines to follow. I would begin by not allowing myself to miss the ball more than 3 times during the play session. (If I failed, I might add the discipline of a half-hour of practice later in the afternoon.) Another time I might demand of myself that I keep my eyes on the ball at all times, that I set myself in a constant ready-position, and that I extend my arm and my whole body fully every time I threw the ball. I didn't bother to tell my companion about my various disciplines. Instead, I adhered to them. They were the banks of the river of my game and they kept the tasks electrified and exciting.

I did almost everything this way. This was not obsessive behavior; it was joy producing. It was exhilarating and inspiring. I gave myself disciplines, goals, and standards that urged me on to excellence. No one knew about them. They were my prods, like having an internal personal trainer. Whenever I achieved my goals or met my standards, new disciplines served to lift me to accomplish the next level of performance as I defined it.

There are some very simple disciplines that you

can put into practice immediately. You might want to:


**Call Yourself to Consciousness**
 Use the alarm on a wristwatch to call your attention at odd times of the day to how you are functioning. When the alarm goes off, immediately ask yourself if you have consciously chosen what you are currently doing or saying.
 Then, make a new choice and observe how your behavior begins to change as a result.
 When you become practiced at this, cease using the alarm and call yourself to consciousness at odd times throughout the day.
 As a result of exercising this discipline, you will begin to realize how seldom you are truly conscious.


 I have often watched people drift off into unconsciousness. They are not even daydreaming, because when they hear their names called, they have no memory of what was holding their attention. They were not present for those moments of life. You would be shocked to discover the accumulated number of years you have passed in this way. Life is precious and deserves your full presence.


**Focus on *What* rather than *Why***
 Throughout every day, pay attention to what

you are doing, saying, and feeling. Observe yourself. Listen to yourself. Be open and compassionate toward yourself.

Do not ask *why*. More important than "Why am I feeling this way?" is "*What* am I feeling?" More meaningful than "Why am I doing this?" is "*What* am I doing and is it appropriate to what I hope to achieve?" More significant than "Why am I saying this?" is "*What* am I saying and does it communicate my experience?"

"What" and "how" lead to creative change and evolution. "Why," results in a meaningless mind-spin.

All too often we analyze and psychologize, *ad nauseam.* We seem fascinated with our explanations, justifications and rationalizations. This is all part of our love affair with talking *about* ourselves rather than focusing on developing into the more we are capable of becoming. If we were good friends to ourselves, the next time we asked "why?" we would answer, "Who cares?"

Most often we explore why we behaved in a particular way because we are concerned with whether we did something wrong or bad. When we assess ourselves as Players, we look to see if what was said or done was an expression of our true selves. Was it in alignment with what we wanted to communicate? Passing judgment does not enter into the evaluation.

## Act One: Who Am I? 33

**Arrive Early and Prepare Yourself**

Woody Allen once said that "80% of success is showing up." You can make a discipline of the other 20% by arriving at least ten minutes early and being prepared. Use the ten minutes to breathe consciously, to shed the tension accrued during the travel time, and to center and align yourself with your purpose for the activity about to begin.

This discipline enables you to enter a scene in a state of wholeness. It affords you the opportunity to be present in a powerful way.

There are two types of performers in the theater, and therefore in life. There is the actor and there is the artist. The actor arrives out-of-breath just before the time he is due at the theater. He hurries into his costume and makeup, all the while thinking about unrelated things. He appears on stage and gives a satisfactory, albeit often superficial and uninspiring, performance. He rushes in and gets by.

The artist, on the other hand, arrives long before her half-hour call. She relaxes, releases the previous activities of the day, and is fully present to her purpose for being in the dressing room. When she begins to prepare for the performance, she merges with the face that is emerging through the makeup and she steps into the character as she steps into the clothing. When she appears on stage she is one with the character and she gives a moving, deeply believable performance. She respects her creativity and the impact of her offering lingers.

These three disciplines will enable you to experience the beginning of immediate changes in the quality of your life and they will give you practice with experiencing yourself as Player.

**Call Yourself to Consciousness**
**Focus on What rather than Why**
**Arrive Early and Prepare Yourself**

## *Exercise:*

Gather a group of friends in your living room for a "theatrical" event. The goal of the evening is for each of you to retain "ownership" of your personality (who you think you are as a character.) To achieve this, you will all participate in a series of auditions for each others' characters.

Here is how it works:

You begin by getting up in front of the group. You tell them a brief touching story from your own life. Your friends listen and carefully observe how you tell the story: your voice, your speed, your intonations, your gestures, your expression of feelings.

You will then sit down and one at a time, two of your friends will "reenact" the touching story you told. They will seek to capture your delivery and to recreate your expression of feelings. Everyone

## Act One: Who Am I?

in the "audience" will observe their embodiment of your presentation.

Then, you will again face the group and tell the same touching story again. Your objective is to tell the story exactly as you told it the first time, using all the same gestures, vocal patterns, and feeling expressions — nothing more, nothing less.

When you finish, the three of you who told the story and played the storyteller will stand before the group which will then vote on who best played the character who made the initial presentation.

In most cases, if you were conscious of your behavior and observant of your original presentation, you will be voted the best performer of "yourself." But beware. One of your friends may watch and listen more closely than you, and present "you" better than you re-presented yourself. The applause for your friend will surpass yours. In that case, it can be said that you lost "your basic character" because someone else played it better, played it more consciously.

This experience will heighten your powers of observation and make you profoundly aware of how you present who you think you are.

As each of you "auditions" for each other, you will have a wealth of experience creating different characters.

## Scene Six
## *What Is Your Motivation?*

You have probably heard jokes about "Method Actors." These performing artists studied the techniques of Constantin Stanislavski, a great Russian acting teacher and Director of the Moscow Art Theatre whose body of work is known in the United States as "the Method." Method actors must feel the truth of the lines they are saying. They don't emote externally. They "believe" what they are doing as the character. If they are given a stage direction, they need to know their motivation for making that move. Directors often pull at their hair because they ask a Method actor to make a cross stage left and the actor is said to ask, "What is my motivation?" The director might then respond, as the joke goes, "Because I need stage right clear for someone's entrance!" The director really wants to shout, "Just do it. If you need a motivation, create your own." It is a point well taken. The actor is responsible for motivating all her moves, all her lines, and all her moments on the stage. She has to know her character's life purpose and her objectives for her presence in the scene at hand.

As this is true for the stage performer, so it is

equally true for each of us. We need to know our life purpose.

To discover what your life purpose might be, review your life to this point to examine the values that have been important to you. To what have you devoted yourself consistently? Where have you invested large amounts of energy? What has held your interest and evoked passion? The answers to these questions will begin to reveal your life purpose because you have been living it out, even if unconsciously.

Here are some examples of life purposes: to love unconditionally; to function with excellence in all circumstances; to serve humanity; to promote peace; to embody creativity. You can see that a life purpose is a broad focus, much larger than a particular goal. It is grand enough to last a lifetime.

Once you identify a life purpose, you can always change and hone the statement of it. Think of it as a "working" life purpose, as in a working title.

Whatever your life purpose might be, if you have it in your consciousness, it will guide you as you make significant choices. If you are devoted to loving unconditionally, you might choose a life in cross-cultural education. If your life purpose is to function with excellence, you might choose difficult and challenging situations in which to prove yourself. Serving humanity might lead you to a career in social services. Promoting peace might make your parenting experience all the more meaningful. Embodying creativity would have you stretching yourself to new artistic expressions in all that you do.

A life purpose serves as the context for your

actions and choices. As Player, when you wake in the morning you need to remind yourself of your purpose for being alive. The minute you do this you stir yourself into meaningful living. Then you choose specific objectives in each life scene where you play a role. These objectives support your ability to stay on course in relation to your life purpose. You begin to develop a throughline of awareness and functioning: from life purpose, to specific objective, to supportive actions, to the awakening of appropriate feelings, to the choice of words, etc.

If, for example, your life purpose is to promote peace, then when you wake in the morning, you remind yourself as you get out of bed that you are a peacemaker. This is what your whole life is truly about. As you start into the day, you might choose as your objective for the day, to listen with sensitivity to what others are saying.

By the time you head to the kitchen for breakfast, you might hear your two teenagers arguing. Rather than allowing yourself to become upset or disgruntled, you would take a deep breath as you make your entrance in the kitchen scene. You would remember that you are Player, and that you can create a character who can embody your life purpose. You would choose a sense of self as mediator and breathe deeply once again to fortify yourself before speaking your first line.

You would remember your objective and begin to listen sensitively to what each of the other characters — in this case your hot and bothered teenagers — is saying. Your first chosen action might be to stand between them. You would direct yourself to

## Act One: Who Am I? 39

cross from the doorway through the chaotic energy that fills the room, to the table where your son and daughter are playing out anger with gusto.

Then you would breathe again. You might reach out to both children, touching them on the shoulders. This would be an invitation to them to calm down, even though you wouldn't say so.

When you begin to verbally engage with them, you would choose dialogue carefully. You would make certain to acknowledge each of them. You would want them both to feel they have been heard, at least by you. You might invite them to talk to you about what is bothering them. As a peacemaker, you would divert their attention from the anger that was flying between them to a more satisfying communication with you, because you, at least, are willing to listen.

You would check your feelings. Because you would be experiencing concern for each of them and sadness that they fight in this way, you would express this to each and both of them. They would probably quiet down a little because they would not want to upset you. As you continue to relate to them, you would activate your objective, listening sensitively to the position of each.

Within a short time, the energy between them would change. There would be room for you to help them do some healing work to restore their love as siblings. You would have lived your life purpose, which is to promote peace.

Maintaining an awareness of purpose is a key factor in remaining conscious. When you do not direct your life on a throughline of unfolding, you can easily drift from one activity to another, devoid of purpose.

I'm sure you have seen actors on stage like this. They seem blank or distant when they have no lines to say. They move about the stage, following the blocking of the director, but their moves seem lifeless.

People function this way on life's stage. You can be in the midst of conversation with someone and even though he may respond, you have the sense that no one is home. His focus is not on what he is saying, what he is hearing, or what he is doing. He is not present. People can live their entire lives that way, without purpose. They eat, sleep, work, play, and then repeat it all the next day. It is as if their original life performance was videotaped and the rest of their days are a rerun. They lack a reason for being. They lack a life purpose.

When you are without purpose, without objectives, you are drawn, as if magnetically, outside of yourself to what others might think of you or want from you. Energy is drawn out of you rather than directed through you.

When you function with purposes and objectives, you empower yourself and direct the course of your life.

I will never forget seeing a profound example of this in a stage performance by Ralph Bellamy. He was playing Franklin Delano Roosevelt in *Sunrise at Campobello*. His purpose as the character was to function at his highest and best in spite of a crippling disease. In the final scene, Roosevelt needed to take a few steps from where he was sitting to a

## Act One: Who Am I?  41

podium in order to deliver a speech. When Bellamy lifted the polio-stricken body he had created, everyone in the audience could feel his purposefulness as he directed his energy into making his legs work. All the other characters on stage were present to him with each step he took.

In the audience, we all watched him and hoped for his success. Simultaneously, we watched ourselves watching and hoping for him. From the stage to the back of the house, it was as if we were one body, one self, seeking to fulfill this goal. It was a simple task that represented a monumental achievement. When he made it to the podium, those on stage and all of us in the audience rose to our feet as one body, cheering. We were all lifted to a new level of accomplishment of the human spirit by those few steps from uncertainty to fruition.

This is what a sense of purpose helps us do in all circumstances: move from uncertainty to fruition.

### *Exercise:*

Use only enough energy to perform any physical movement; excess energy use results in unnecessary tension. To determine if excess is involved, try simple things such as lifting your arm or standing on one leg. Are you creating tension elsewhere in your body that is not needed to perform these tasks? If yes, then breathe in and on the exhale release the excess tension.

Lie on the floor and roll slowly to the other side of the room. Don't push yourself over, that creates excess. Instead, direct your body to begin to move and let your own body weight pull in you in the direction you are going. With each roll, release more and more superfluous tension.

### *Exercise:*

Move a chair from one side of the room to other. Then, move it back again.

Do the same task, but this time give yourself a strong purpose for moving the chair. See if you can experience the difference in your focus and determination with and without a purpose.

If you are going for an interview or you want to make a sale or you want a favor from a friend, give yourself a specific purpose for the task. Make it important to you. Back it up with objectives and activities. For example, you want your friend to lend you $1,000. That is your goal. Your purpose is different from the goal. Your purpose might be to give yourself peace of mind. As you can see, this is larger than the specific goal. Your objective (what you want) could be to alleviate a crisis in your home. Your activities (what you do to get what you want) could be: to convince your friend, to develop the confidence to ask, to breathe deeply and calm yourself, to open yourself to all possibilities, etc.

If you have a purpose and you act on it, you will more easily guide yourself through every life experience.

## Scene Seven
## *Truthfulness*

Stanislavski taught his actors to act truthfully with a purpose. Prior to his influence, many actors romped about the stage posturing. Their acting was external. They pretended that they were feeling something rather than actually feeling. Stanislavski stressed realness. He knew that when the actor experienced what he was acting, the audience would experience it with him. This would result in tremendous theatrical gratification, such as the powerful moment in *Sunrise at Campobello.*

As Players in life, one of our main tasks is to act truthfully with adherence to our chosen life purpose. It is not for us to be true to an outer calling, to someone else's wishes. As Shakespeare said, "To thine own self be true" and it will follow that we cannot be false to anyone. We must be true to what we know is right for us in any given moment.

Living truthfully means not compromising because it is expedient. If, in the midst of a conversation with a friend, you experience discomfort because you heard a racist comment, you would not be living truthfully if you did not express your dismay. To be truthful, you would have to experience and acknowledge your discomfort and take issue with the statement.

If a feeling of love fills you in the midst of an exchange with another, it would be important for you to find the right expression for that feeling of love. Your objective would be to embody the feeling and also to make it known to the other.

If you feel an impulse to do something, make the impulse manifest in action as soon as possible. A delay might diminish the power of what rose in you. By the time you would later pay it heed, the impulse might take a lesser form which wouldn't express what you originally awakened.

If you are not functioning truthfully with a purpose, you may resort to cliché ways of behaving. Something goes wrong and before you have a chance to make a conscious response, you groan "Oh no," throw your hands on your forehead, and send your eyes heavenward. While the gesture is fine and does communicate because it is so recognizable, it does not represent what your true feelings are in that moment. You are not choosing a fresh response.

So often you are asked how you are, and you often brush off the question with, "I'm fine." You deny yourself the chance to hear the question in that moment and touch a true response. You never discover how you are and you don't share that with the one asking.

Your focus should not be on impressing others. Your obligation is to be true to self and to choose how to share that truth with others. If you know the truth and you share a lesser version or a lie through your character expression, then your life becomes a lie. You don't speak truth because you are cowardly, or because you determine in advance what you think will please others and then you tailor your response to your projection. You don't speak truth because you have been untrue to yourself for so long that you don't know how.

Children are, for the most part, a segment of the population that still remembers how to speak truth. I recall a father and son playing on the same side of a doubles tennis match. The father, after committing an inappropriate move, said to his son, "I hope it was all right with you that I crossed over in front of you and hit that shot." The boy responded, "Well, actually, no!" Most adults would have said, "No problem" even if they considered the move offensive.

A classic example of a child's integrity occurred on an airplane. I was in the window seat and a young boy was on the aisle. The person in the middle dropped a stinker of a fart. It was powerful enough to be fully experienced in the rows in front of us and behind us. The adults occupying those seats made no visible reaction. However, the boy on the aisle lifted his head and nose and began sniffing all around. Locating the culprit on his right, he screwed up his face in an appropriate expression of distaste and emitted a loud "peeuw" sound that clearly indicated his displeasure. His spontaneous and honest response provoked a spontaneous response in the "farter" who laughed with relief.

Whereas children are often not self-conscious, most adults are busy protecting each other from the facts of living.

In addition to being true to yourself, never limit yourself to who you think you are. You are always more than you think you are. You may not know this because you have spent so much of your life playing the same role over and over every day. Expand your repertoire. Try new ways of being and practice being true to self within that new way of being.

## *Exercise:*

Give yourself the challenge of moving differently in and through your body. Begin walking back and forth in your "own" walk. Be aware of how you hold yourself, what part of your body seems to lead, whether you have excess tension, etc. See if you can determine where your "center" is located. Is it your head that is pulling you forward? Do your shoulders or knees drag you ahead? Is your chest or stomach the predominant focal point?

Once you determine this, use imaginative images to shift your center and see what it does to your walk and how it makes you feel. For example, place an imaginary 5-carat ruby in your belly button and begin to walk. See what it does to your hip movements, let alone to your attitude about yourself. Or, place an imaginary heavy barbell on your shoulders, or warm butter melting down your spine, or bricks in your shoes, or feathers inside your head, or jelly in your calves.

The more changes you can make in your movements, the more you will open to a world of vast potential.

## *Exercise:*

Observe how someone on the street is walking and shift your own walk to match his/hers. Be aware of the effect on you both physically and in your feeling nature. Or, observe someone in a restaurant who eats differently from the way you do. Practice eating in this new way and see how you feel about yourself.

Choose a characteristic in a loved one that distresses you. Experience this characteristic from the inside out by embodying it. In this way you will be on the inside of another's behavior and you will gain valuable insights.

Or, choose behavior in another that you greatly admire but never thought you were capable of doing. Experience this behavior from the inside out. You may discover that you have simply been denying or delaying potential in yourself to be more than you thought you were.

## *In Summary*

One of the quickest ways to awaken yourself to consciousness in any given moment is to remind yourself to ask the question, "Who am I?" This jars you out of patterned functioning and into remembering that you are Player making choices of behavior and response. When you remember who you are, you can turn your attention to what you are doing. What are your purposes and objectives? What are you bringing into being?

You are the inventor of your own life. You live something out and say that it is real. You say, "I am unhappy." You believe that this is true and in fact you are unhappy. You say that if this and that were to change you could be happy. You are creating the entire reality. Someone else might step into your very circumstance and proclaim this situation reason to be happy. They might say, "If any of this were to change, I might not be as happy." Who is correct? Both of you are. Each is inventing life and responses to life. What is real is what you believe is real.

I remember the evening when I had gathered with several adults for a social time. One was the almost 40-year-old son of two other guests. During the pleasant, uneventful evening, the son left the room saying he needed to call his wife. Those of us remaining in the room gave his remark no special importance and continued our conversation. The son was gone for a very long time. He returned as if nothing had happened, and we responded to him in kind because we had not been focused on him during his absence.

Several days later we discovered that the son had been having an anxiety attack and didn't know if he could make it through the evening with his parents. He called his wife for support and spent a good part of his time on the phone sobbing. None of us had any idea that this was transpiring. We had no indication of any problem before, during, or after.

## Act One: Who Am I? 49

What was very clear was that the son had created a powerful reality of despair and it was unmistakably real for him. As far as I could tell, and I am quite observant, nothing said or done had provoked the son's feeling of non-safety. It all resided within him. Whatever he heard, or thought he heard, he used to inflict pain upon himself. He shifted his consciousness into identification with debilitating character patterns and he disempowered himself.

What the son did that evening, many of us do to ourselves constantly. We forget who we are and we become victims of our own unconsciousness.

The most important first step toward functioning consciously and powerfully is to know Who You Are. To know "I Am Player" is to open the way to all possibilities in every moment.

## *A Major Experience for Activating Player Creativity and Bringing a New Character into Being*

Gather a large array of clothing for both genders and all ages, including shoes, hats, scarves, and accessories. Lay them all out in your largest room so that each piece is visible to you. As you distribute them, consider that you are creating the Creator's Costume Shop and that each item represents a different characteristic or quality from which you can choose to bring into being (out of whole cloth) a new personality through which to interact in the world.

Prepare yourself for the new by standing in the

center of the costume shop, breathing into how you have always thought of yourself, and holding the intention to release all that you have been and to open to the new.

Slowly remove all that you are currently wearing, one article at a time, including jewelry and eye glasses. With each removal, focus on letting go of this quality from your personality. Place each item in front of you, building a small pile of "the old self." When you are stripped bare of the past, pick up the pile of "who you were" and take it just outside the costume shop. Re-enter and breathe into the intention to be led to totally new characteristics and ways of being.

Allow yourself to be drawn (don't decide in your mind what looks good or what would feel good) to whatever speaks to you. Put it on, either as how it was meant to be worn or in ways that simply feel right. For example, you might tie pant legs around your neck and wear it as a cape because that is what your intuition directs. Continue to roam about in the costume shop adding only those items that speak to you and feel good once you have put them on. With each addition, yield to what it calls forth in you, even if that is totally unfamiliar. This is a process of discovery, of becoming someone new.

Experience the emerging character and register how it feels to be this. How do you walk? Or sit? Or stand? How do you speak? Do you have a different voice? What attitudes or feelings are awakened in you? Take time to be present as this new character. Move about in the newly created self, making sure that you are observing the differences between

## Act One: Who Am I?  51

who you were and who you have become.

Then walk in the new self to retrieve the pile representing your old self. Pick it up, bring it to the center of the room and put it down in front of you.

Close your eyes and breathe into the new creation, experiencing it one more time. Slowly begin to remove the articles that have gone into creating this new expression. Be aware of the changes that occur as you remove each one. Release all the articles (characteristics) and stand naked in your real self, Player, Player who brings the character into being.

Reflecting on all the articles (characteristics) that made up the new character, determine which one item, more than all the others, is the essence of the new, the single factor that gave birth to what you created. Open your eyes, reach down, select this article and put it to the side.

Slowly begin to put on who you used to be, one item at a time. As you do this be aware that you are not simply returning to who you used to be, but rather you are choosing each of these qualities and creating them as your character. You are Player, giving life to this (re)emerging personality. Consciously recreate who you used to be. Feel the power that comes of conscious creation, for then you will know that you indeed are the creator and that you have the ability to make changes whenever you wish.

After you are "reconstructed," gather all the materials in the costume shop and put them away.

Stand in the center of the cleared room with the single article from the created character in front of you. Walk about the room in your familiar self, speaking aloud and moving as you always have in the past. Realize that you are consciously doing this, creating this.

Then pick up the single article and put it on. As you do, allow all the new characteristics to flood in and take over. Move in the new character and be aware of the differences between the new and the old. Delight in your creativity and your ability to be a completely different "person" by choice.

Now you have a direct experience of knowing "Who Am I?" You are Player who brings character into being.

# ACT TWO

# *How Am I?*
# *Creating an Environment*
# *for Becoming*

"It is not possible to create an environment for becoming if character is on automatic pilot. When I am not fully present, change (through spontaneity and creativity) does not happen."
— *Maureen McCready, Buffalo, NY*

"The major key for me is trust in myself to stay on the throughline and my expression is then congruent with what I am registering."
— *Sandra Coyne, Aurora, OH*

"Focusing on an objective keeps me aligned with the throughline. The process is important, not the finished product. I can bring something different into being by letting go of what I think I already know, by letting go of planning, and by listening to what wants expression."
— *Shirley Routliffe, Victoria, BC*

"I learned through experience the difference between thinking about an appropriate action and directing myself with feeling from my center in movement and on the throughline. This life is a play and consciousness is the awareness that we are playing ourselves."
— *James Stavoy, San Francisco, CA*

"The public solitude experience was created by acting on impulses, making something start to happen, and extending the line of action as authentically as possible. I acknowledged resistance and self-consciousness as it occurred and plowed through it with an act of will."
— *Linda Reisser, Portland, OR*

"I have been given a tool kit of 'hows,' the 'hows' of consciously bringing myself to the moment. When I experienced the energy moving through me I became the receptacle for the Divine. I was free – the Power to Create. It was like a wash of holy molecules flowing down. This was a coming home."
— *Antara Scales, Manhattan Beach, CA*

"I learned how to pinpoint an objective once I have a purpose, and how important it is to choose a quality through which to fan out the Life Force needed to attain this objective."
— *Fernand Villemure, Sainte Foy, QC*

## Scene One
## *Creating an Inner Environment for Becoming*

Once you begin to know who you are, you can turn your attention to the scenery of your life. You can become the "set designer," creating an inner and outer environment to enhance the process of becoming. You can learn how to make the body more responsive to your direction, and how to strengthen your concentration. You can begin to practice the liberating art of "public solitude."

Your purpose is to encourage your spiritual growth and to embody more of your potential. To facilitate this process, it is essential to consciously create both an inner and an outer environment for becoming.

There are several key areas to develop consciously when creating your inner environment. They are
- Your thinking mind
- Your physical body
- Your feeling self
- Your communication skills

- Your intuition

These areas need to be positive on all scores. You need to weed out what doesn't serve your process of becoming and replace the negative or debilitating aspects with qualities that are positive and creative.

## *Your Thinking Mind*

The most all pervasive environment in which you live is the world of your thoughts. If you prefer thinking things through, thinking about life, holding opinions, and logically determining how to proceed in any given moment, you are like many others who dwell excessively on the mental level. Males tend to be even more extreme in this regard.

Save your energy. Don't waste it by creating worry about impending interactions, worry about tomorrow, and worry about the future. Discipline your mind to remain in the now moment. Use it to report on what is actually transpiring. Train it to be factual rather than foreboding.

When you function through your mind, refrain from attributing motives to other people and convincing yourself that you are correct. Laugh at how humorous this practice is.

Do not inundate yourself with negative thoughts; fill your mind with positive thoughts and teach yourself to live lightly. Be aware whenever you attempt to think yourself out of a horrendous situation that has not even occurred. Trying to prob-

## Act Two: How Am I? 57

lem solve when there is no problem is like trying to name your baby when you are not yet even pregnant. Remain in the present, seeking opportunities in problems that are actually occurring.

Your thoughts include your opinions. Do you hold them fiercely and defend them at all costs? Let me burst your bubble. The truth is that opinions are relatively worthless and affect nothing. Don't cling to them and most certainly don't try to impose them on others.

Beliefs are also residents of the mind and arbitrary. If you insist on holding them, don't invest energy in getting friends and family to join you.

To enhance the process of becoming, use your mental faculties to good ends in problem-solving, in dreaming up solutions and ways to advance yourself, in careful planning, and in structuring your life.

The key question is: are you in charge of your mind or does the mind control you? If the mind controls you, you use it to build frameworks for how you experience the world and then say, "That is the reality." You proceed to live in that box and call it proof that that is the way things are.

You can expand your mind, and therefore your inner growth, by opening your mind to multiple possibilities in all areas. Whenever you think of one useful thing, demand of yourself that you think of at least three others as well. This will stretch you beyond any self-imposed limitations.

### Exercises:

1. Write a description of a loved one. Then write three more totally different descriptions of the same person, seeking to capture even more of the person.
2. Instead of just working a cross-word puzzle, create one.
3. Choose an historical or a political figure you object to strongly. Make a list of at least ten positive attributes or strengths of this person.
4. Look at a current problem in your life. Bring into your awareness three people who are different from you in personality and general approach to life. You don't need to agree with them or even to like them. Step inside each of the three, as if you were playing their character instead of your own, and see what they think about your problem. Borrow what works for you and apply it to your problem.

### Your Physical Body

Your physical body is often run by the negative mind, especially in the ways you limit your movements. You convince yourself of what you can and can't do. However, if your body is more responsive to your conscious direction, you can effectively create a more supportive environment for becoming. You can improve your health, live longer and better, use your physical vehicle for creativity, and learn to excel. When you have creative jurisdiction over your body, you can lead it in movement, development

## Act Two: How Am I?  59

and shape, and it will serve as the perfect housing for your expanding spirit.

The physical body can surprise you with feats you didn't think possible and therefore encourage you to expressions of consciousness you also didn't think were possible.

The physical body is your vehicle of expression and it is important that it be congruent with what is transpiring within. If it is, you remain aligned with your emergence in spirit.

So often, on the tennis court, I will tell myself, "Naah, I can't make that shot." When I do that, I stop myself before I even try for it. On the occasions that I surpass my own negative judgment, I discover with great delight that I can not only move my body to where the ball is landing, but I can actually hit the ball as I choose to hit it and direct it to the other side of the court. This kind of surpassing and embodying stretches me to become more than I thought I was and the body enables me to prove that through its actions.

### *Exercises:*

1. Practice loving your physical body by standing in front of a mirror, preferably naked. Instead of judging your body with negative mind comments, invite your body to speak to you. Let it tell you all the good things about itself.

2. Perform a physical activity, such as swimming, tennis, or golf, and as you play, direct yourself consciously throughout each movement. In this way

you will add conscious jurisdiction to what might be familiar rote movement. You will create an inner relationship to outer physical movement, enhancing your inner environment for becoming.

## *Your Feeling Self*

Your feeling self is a power center in the process of evolving. Feeling is the fire that fuels your sense of knowing that something is true. Feeling is the passion with which the new is created and sustained. When you function unconsciously, you think you *have* feelings, rather than know that you *create* them. When you think you have them, you are had by them! We will deal with this concept fully in Act Three.

If you were taught early on in your life to squelch your feelings, now is the time to unleash them. First you have to become reacquainted with them. You may have suppressed them so successfully that you no longer know that the feeling center is alive. Your feelings may have been completely co-opted by your thoughts. Listen to yourself speak when someone asks you what you are feeling. If you say, "I think I am feeling..." then you are not feeling, you are thinking.

The development of your inner environment will be greatly enriched by the awakening and conscious direction of your feelings. You will be enlivened and moved to action. Feelings get your "juices" flowing, add a glow to your skin, and heighten your awareness of everything around you.

## *Exercise:*

Put a photograph of a loved one in front of you. Look into the person's face and allow yourself to feel, to feel fully. Monitor that you are not drifting into thinking thoughts about this person. Feel. If the feelings become merged with memories that you shared with this person, go into the memories and relive the feelings of then or be aware of how you feel now about that time together. Write down a few images or metaphors that convey what you are feeling; for example, I feel warm and tender, as if drenched in high-noon sunlight. Or, I feel as if I were tucked beneath a down comforter. Note how the feelings wash over the whole of you and bring you to more animated expression.

Look again at the photograph. This time simply write a description of what you see with your eyes, without awakening feeling. Note how flat and uninteresting this expression is when compared with the journey you just took into feelings.

## *Your Communication Skills*

As you proceed, remember that we are functioning in a theatre metaphor. The stage is an encapsulated version of life that is happening powerfully in the moment. In a play the characters have very specific words they speak. They don't ad lib, they don't put in extras, they speak the exact words they were given to speak and they have a minimal amount of latitude in terms of their physical movements. They are to be alive and natural and spontaneous, but they have been directed to be in a particular place at a particular time. This is not just for convenience so that actors don't run into each other. This is because the director was present, staging the event to get the most power out of a given moment. There are no wasted motions, no wasted words. The power is carried on the throughline. If it is dissipated in any way, it takes away from the essence of what is being put forth.

In life, the same is true. To sharpen your communication skills, choose the words you speak carefully and consciously. Don't ramble. Don't engage in excess. Direct yourself to imprint those around you with chosen words and actions. Hold an objective of entering the essence of what you seek to communicate and speak from the center of that essence.

To effectively create an inner environment for becoming, always have a purpose for your actions and interactions. That purpose guides and directs what you choose to say and how you say it. When you function this way you will not only give life to your purpose but you will be sharp, succinct, powerful, and impactful because your energy will flow from you as on a narrow beam of penetrating light.

The effect on your inner environment will be a strong sense of alignment. What you meant will line up perfectly with what you are communicating.

## Exercise:

Think of a favor you would like to ask of a friend. Choose two friends for this practice. With the first friend, put forth your request in a roundabout way. Hint at what you want but don't say it directly. For example, let's say you want to ask your friend to baby-sit your pet for a day. In the indirect approach you might say, "I'm going to attend a presentation on Saturday. I don't like leaving my dog alone for all those hours. But (quickly interjected) I'm sure he will be OK." Then go on with a long story about having left him alone before and what happened. Then, "I don't suppose you are free on Saturday." If your friend says, "Yes," say, "You wouldn't really want to spend your free day watching my dog, would you?" Etc. You get the idea. In this exchange you are rambling and mostly issuing a negative presentation. It is as if you are protecting yourself from a response of "No." Whatever response you get from your friend, be conscious of what is transpiring in you as you ramble. Note how powerless you are, how weak and ineffectual.

With your second friend, say, "I need a sitter for my dog on Saturday. Can you do it?" Feel the difference: no excess, no unnecessary elaboration, no whining, no manipulation — just a simple clear statement and question. See what comes back as a response, but more importantly, be aware of how it felt to communicate from a straight line within yourself and a clear purpose.

## *Your Intuition*
Developing your intuition is one of the most important things you can do to further enhance your inner environment for becoming. Your intuition is your voice of inner knowing. Intuition connects directly with the greater wisdom that abounds and it enables you to hear it and use it for your greater good.

Intuition is called by many names: premonition, hunch, or feeling. It sometimes just slips into your awareness. Or, it may speak to you as a booming voice that demands your attention. Intuition tells you what you need to know and what to do. To strengthen it all you need to do is listen to it and do what it says. In that sense it is akin to a muscle; the more you use it the more powerful it gets.

## *Exercise:*
The next time you are confronted with a decision, after asking yourself what you think you should do, ask yourself what you sense you might do. This will help you separate thinking from feeling and give you practice with touching your intuition.

When you want something, ask instead "What is wanted of me?" The answer resides in the intuition, in the connection to spirit and all that is larger than the character.

## Scene Two
## *Concentration*

Concentration contributes greatly to creating an inner environment for becoming. It is the ability to function purposefully, undistracted, unruffled, and unshakable. The more focused you can be in any given moment, the more influence you can have on your character interaction in the world. When you develop concentration, you can begin every life moment from the center of consciousness (or the consciousness of centeredness.) Can you begin to feel what this means? You are in the moment and fully present to what is transpiring. You are not distracted by other people or noises or scents or even your own thoughts. This lack of distraction facilitates your establishing an inner silent chamber where the forces of creativity can work harmoniously to bring the new into being.

From this centeredness you expand to incorporate the unfolding scene into your awareness. You don't jump out of yourself, pulled by what others are doing or saying. When you practice concentration, you stand inside your very being and bring the outer in so that you remain centered and whole when you expand. The reverse of this can lead to loss of self, to confusion, even to chaos.

Suppose you are having a serious conversation with a loved one and the other person begins to shout and become angry. If you go outside of yourself you will be drawn into his or her energy and scramble in your mind to think of what to say. You become a victim or allow the other person's anger to awaken your own because you stepped outside of self. But if, when the other begins to shout, you bring that person into the stability of your own centeredness, then when you respond to him/her you are able to respond from strength, without excess, and without getting caught in the anger the other is sending. The words you say will carry power enough to embrace his/her disturbance and even quiet it.

This kind of concentration requires energy. Energy is generated by breathing deeply and by focusing on the life force that is available.

You can also strengthen the inner environment for becoming by directing your attention to creating an outer environment that supports concentration. It might be helpful for you to take stock of your home and work surroundings to see what enhances your consciousness. What distracts, detracts, or invites unconsciousness? What changes can you make immediately?

In my own life, silence, surrounding beauty, and spaciousness enhance my consciousness. Clutter on my desk, noisy music, drips in the sink, clothing lying around, and undone dishes are all distractions. Too many items on my agenda for the day invite unconsciousness because part of me is trying to get away from the overload. Doing things that don't please me or doing things without a defined purpose often leads to unconsciousness. I do them but I am not fully present; I am not concentrating and therefore I am not powerfully directing my energy through a specific intention.

## *Exercise:*

Give names and descriptions to patterns or triggers in you that cause you to be pulled out of your centered state in response to events or interactions with others. Once you name them, you invite yourself to have greater jurisdiction over them.

Identify what disenables you from remaining conscious, what disturbs your concentration, and what drains you of your creative power.

*For example*, I have a "righteous self." If someone falsely accuses me of something and I am not functioning consciously, I quickly get pushed out of shape and immediately retaliate. When I am conscious, I might simply say, "I don't know that to be true of me." It releases me from getting my feelings fired up and needing to make a defensive response.

Remind yourself often that you are Player who brings the character into being, not the reverse. When you remember you are Player you are in charge of your choices. You can guide yourself to concentrate fully on the present moment. You can call yourself to awareness and experience that you are functioning consciously and you are not victim of the moment.

There are ways of identifying when you are functioning as Player. Player doesn't talk; it urges. Player infuses the manifested form known as character with life energy. This is how it urges. As Player you make a commitment to expressing power by infusing the character with life force for its functioning.

Player is constantly becoming the more of who it is. Characters prefer pre-set characteristics in order to feel secure and under control. Others also prefer that we are crystallized as characters and predictable. Player is unpredictable even to self. Each life moment requires concentration and focus on what is emerging and who of you is emerging.

## Scene Three
## *Expanding Concentration from the Inside Out*

When your personality (your instrument) is not prepared (disciplined) for creative work, you lack concentration. You are like a limp string on a violin offering yourself to a virtuoso for playing. With concentration you can establish artistic and creative jurisdiction over your life.

In order to shift your attention away from how others may think of you, shift your attention within and function from the inner.

Actors on stage play out to the audience through a make-believe fourth wall, the proscenium opening to the house (the auditorium). They create that fourth wall in their imagination as if it were a part of the scenery and then they play through it. They begin in the inner self of the character they are creating and project outward, never to the audience directly, but through the fourth wall to the audience.

In life we also need a fourth wall so that we may remain centered while coming forth. We create a fourth wall with an imaginary circle of attention that we draw to differentiate our inner environment from the outer environment.

## *Exercise:*

You might like to try a **Circle of Attention** experience. In this experience you will learn about functioning in solitude in public. No matter where you are or who might be present, you can create a small circle of attention and be in solitude in the midst of others or anything.

Call together a small group of friends with whom you can practice.

**Part One:** In a large room, set up a chair and a small table with an illumined lamp on it. Select a few personal items to place on the floor just beyond the table (creating, in effect, the end of your "stage" and the beginning of the audience). The circle of light falling from the lamp will delineate your small circle of attention. Your friends will sit just beyond your designated circle.

Choose one of three things about which to speak aloud to yourself as you sit in the chair:

1. A deeply moving experience, or
2. A cause about which you feel strongly, or
3. A dilemma you are working with right now as a problem or challenge.

Your task is to stay focused on what you are exploring and to hold your attention within your tiny environment, without being distracted by your friends or saying anything for their sake. Don't reach beyond the "fourth wall" of your small circle to accommodate them. Hold your concentration on what you are saying, feeling, and thinking and on the details of your tiny environment (the table, the light, the objects in front of you).

*Remember:* this small circle represents *you* when you are at home in your core of self. Always start from where you experience yourself, not from where you think you should be or where anyone else wants you to be. The voice of your own director will place you appropriately on the stage of your life.

When you are alone in the smallest circle of self, you are in solitude. When you expand out, you always begin from within that smallest circle and then extend into the public or larger field of interaction by going "through" the fourth wall of your circle of attention. Public solitude refers to functioning always and ever from that still point of knowing and then expanding it outward into life. If you are whole in yourself you can expand outward to become one with others. You can't expand outward if you are divided in self.

Begin speaking from within your small circle of light.

When you finish this first phase, ask your friends for feedback about how well you held your concentration and share your own experience with them. If you were pulled out of your center of awareness at any time, see if you can determine the cause so that you can have jurisdiction over this at another time.

As a way of gaining greater clarification in relation to Player and character, answer this question for yourself: When I talk to myself, who is speaking to whom?

**Part Two:** Expand from the small circle into a larger one, about five feet beyond the first circle. Add throw pillows and a few more objects at the new "fourth wall" line. Have your friends move back to that line.

Start in the chair of the first circle, speaking about the same thing you just explored verbally. As you speak, rise from the chair and begin moving in the larger environment you have created. Be aware that this larger circle still represents your inner environment. Practice staying attentive and purposeful within the permitted area, relating to the objects if you wish, but remaining most aware of your inner life and the fact that you are talking to yourself in public solitude. You know the audience is out there. The important question is: are you centered in yourself or are you distracted by those outside yourself? As you speak, experience yourself expanding, from the inside out.

When you finish ask your friends for feedback on your concentration. Reflect on how you can give yourself greater inner and outer space to become, or how you can enhance your space for becoming. Share your reflections with your friends and discuss the process thus far.

**Part Three:** Expand the circle one last time, another five feet, adding objects, and creating a new "fourth wall" line. Begin again with the same verbal exploration in the chair and this time, expand into the entire larger space. Remember concentration. It is a zeroing in, a way of focusing. Become intimate with what you see in your created space so as not to become intimidated by it. Fill the space with the whole of yourself. Expand your movements and your voice volume as you expand your attention out from a single point only as far as you can go without going past yourself.

When your attention begins to waver, pull back in. For centering, always redirect to a single point and enlarge again from that point.

When you finish the exploration, get feedback from your friends. Then reflect on what you have discovered as your greatest distractions, those you use to hamper your daily concentration. You might also look at how you stop yourself from feeling.

Later ask yourself, if I were to shift more into Player and even farther from identification with character, what do I envision awaits me as a different way to be living in the world? As you answer this question, see if you can begin to embody the new that is forming.

## Scene Four
## *Conscious Reality Creation and Choice Making*

"Life" is our own invention. As in a play, life is a series of "ifs" and "given circumstances" thought up by us. There is as little actuality to life as there is in a made-up play. Life-art is the product of our imagination.

In the midst of a "real life scene" we are influenced by the external circumstances (the setting, the people present, or an event taking place). That is the outer environment in which we are living. We are aware of energy moving within ourselves which guides our responses or actions. That is our inner environment for becoming.

Let's say you are at a party. Many characters are interacting. One fellow is overly loud and drawing attention to himself. In observing the external circumstances you hear the noise and notice the different reactions from the people in the room. Based on the external you might make the choice to join him in his antics, seek to quiet him down, ignore him, etc. When you turn your attention to energy registry within yourself as you observe the noisy fellow, you might experience what is transpiring beneath the outburst: sadness, insecurity, or fear. Based on this registry you might respond very differently: with caring, with empathy, or with a gesture of physical steadying.

In order to choose how you will respond, you must be functioning consciously. To know if you are functioning consciously you should always be able to answer four questions: Who, where, what, how.

> **Who** am I in this moment; what sense of self is present?
> **Where** have I just come from physically and in thought and feeling?
> **What** am I doing here? What do I want? (This leads to action.)
> **How** shall I express myself?

You may be wondering who stops to reflect on these four questions when at a party. The answer is not many people. But then, not many are focused on creating their own reality, on consciously playing their role on the stage of the party. Too often we prefer to be swept along with whatever is happening. The externals dominate our lives.

If, however, you want to function with power, if you want to live a creative life, and if you want to have an impact on your world, then you will take the time to know the answer to those four questions. They will help create your inner environment and affect how you respond to your outer environment for becoming.

## *Exercise:*

Try this right now (if the timing is appropriate). Call someone on the phone, just to say hello and have casual conversation for a while. You know, "how are you, what are you doing?" etc. Observe yourself. I suspect you will find that the prevailing tide of the conversation will carry you along through a mundane interaction.

After you hang up, answer the four questions for yourself. Come up with a sense of self (such as "the eager beaver," "the helpful friend," "the sexy lady," "the warrior," etc.)

Now check out what you are thinking and feeling as a result of making the call.

Then, choose another person to call, but decide before you do, "What do I want during this conversation? What do I want to do? What do I want to achieve?"

Then decide how you will express yourself as you speak. Will you be forceful, gentle, alluring, clever, etc.?

Combine all four aspects: your sense of self, what you are thinking and feeling, what you want, and how you will express yourself. Make the call and observe yourself. I suspect you will be surprised by the imprint you make, by the way the conversation unfolds because of your influence, by the strength you feel through functioning consciously, and by the response you get from the other.

## Scene Five
## *How Am I?*

When you are self-conscious it is because you cease to be present to yourself, not because others are present and possibly focused on you. You don't function well if you leave yourself. Not functioning well is not the result of what anyone else is doing or being.

You create an environment for becoming through concentration.

### *Exercise:*

Try this practice with a few friends. You serve as the leader of the experience. Choose three objects. Place one of them in the center of your circle. Have your friends observe the object for 30 seconds. Then have them close their eyes and report on what they saw.

After everyone reports, have everyone open their eyes to see what they all remembered or didn't remember.

Do the same thing with a second object in 20 seconds and then with the third object in 10 seconds.

Then ask them to close their eyes immediately and say what someone else in the room is wearing that they noticed and remembered. Still with eyes closed, call on them to say what a specific someone is wearing. Have them open their eyes and report.

This should provide many laughs and reveal much about concentration.

Immediately ask them to close their eyes again and this time have each of them report on what he or she is wearing. You will all be surprised by how many people pay little attention to their own choice of clothing for the day.

Exercises like this sharpen our concentration skills.

**You create an environment for becoming through concentration, but also through freedom.**

Freedom does not come from outside of yourself. Therefore your freedom is also not affected by anything that is going on outside of yourself. Player is always free to make choices but is often limited or restricted in character, by character. It's a dictatorship in, of, and by character. All too often, past history determines "How Am I." You need freedom from the past history of the character. Your character is not chained to what has happened to it. Like your body when not restricted by the mind, your character has freedom of movement and becoming when not restricted by the past.

## Exercise:

To get a feeling for this, put on music that has a chaotic beat and allow your body to move in unfamiliar ways.

Next, add conscious choice to this by breathing out through the heart center. See how this affects your movement to this same music.

Your point of focus, of concentration, directly affects what you hear, what you say, what you receive, what you create.

You need to learn to do whatever you do with consciousness, whether sitting, walking, speaking etc. To be attentive and to appear attentive are two different things. You are either real or imitative. Talking without focus or moving hands and feet mechanically is the antithesis of functioning with discrimination. To really look and to really see any object holds the viewer's attention as well as the attention of others. It points them to what you want them to look at. Hence, if you are centered in a particular frequency, you will have a far better chance of drawing another to the matching frequency.

## Exercise:

For further insight, the next time you are out with a friend, begin talking, strictly from your head, about what you wish was different in the world. Use opinions and thoughts only and see what this evokes in your friend. My guess is that you will get opinions and thoughts back.

Mid stream, shift your attention to the solar plexus and generative centers (the belly of feelings and the genital area below that). Allow passion to fill your discourse on your wishes and begin sharing what you see to do about this. Observe what happens in your friend and what comes back to you. I suspect you will be met with matching energy.

Creating an environment for becoming requires that you be observant, that you look at everything in new ways, and that you allow yourself to express feelings. Try the following to give you practice with this.

## *Exercise:*

Look in the mirror for five full minutes. Be present with as few thoughts as possible. What do you observe that you have not seen before? What do you feel about what you are discovering?

Close your eyes. Bring into your consciousness the face and personality of a loved one. Just be present to the face of the loved one, with as few thoughts as possible. What do you observe that you have not seen before? What do feel about what you are discovering?

Sustaining and maintaining consciousness need not be a major effort. You can do it by sharpening your awareness in the moment and then carrying that awareness to the next moment and the next.

## Act Two: How Am I? 81

Consciousness then becomes a long sequence of individual moments of being fully present. As Player you infuse character with the desire and the energy to remain aware and awake.

When you are awake, you don't fall into false realities where you believe that things are the way they are. Nothing is fixed, everything is in flux and all things are possible. But when you get caught in the web of group thinking, belief systems, and patterned ways of functioning, you forget that you are creating the reality in which you are stuck.

You are always inventing fictions. When you are conscious, you know you are inventing them. When you are unconscious, you forget and you get trapped. When conscious, you are like a farmer. You plant the seeds of your imagination in the ground. You harvest real physical representations and because you have made them visible, you can relate to them. All the while, you are cognizant of the "make believe."

Don't think that "make believe" is limited to actors or to children. All our lives are "make believe."

The whole creative process is guided, when you are conscious, by your inner sense of truth that enables you to know when you are on course.

Have you ever said: I'm the kind of person who...? Whatever you tack on the end of that statement is what you believe. It is your "make believe" version of how you see yourself. In fact, you don't have to be the kind of person who ... anything. Or you can be the kind of person who ... everything. All you have to do is choose. Try it right now.

*Exercise:*

Choose a quality you don't often express but that you've seen in another, something you would like to incorporate but is, as yet, unexpressed or underdeveloped in you. Settle on that quality. Breathe it in. Let's say the quality is boisterous enthusiasm. Think of something you did in the last little while that you feel good about. Now, call someone you know on the phone and after the initial niceties, burst right into a telling of what you feel good about. Be sure to give full life to boisterous enthusiasm.

Observe how it feels. See what kind of feedback you get. Be aware that you just created this quality. You are now the kind of person who is boisterously enthusiastic. You are the author of this life fiction.

Try the reverse. Choose a quality you would not want to express. How about, painfully shy? Breathe into this. See how it feels. How does it change the way you hold your body, the way you look out through your eyes? Take out a sheet of paper and begin a letter to someone you love. Through painful shyness try to express how you feel. Observe yourself carefully. Look at the size of the letters, look at the words you have chosen, and watch how you hold yourself back. You are the author of this fiction as well.

The answer to the question How Am I? is: however I choose to be. Remember every option is a

## Act Two: How Am I?    83

possibility if you are conscious and know that as Player you can bring anything into being through your character.

When you live in the "that's the way it is" or "this is who I am" mode, that is where you remain encased. And that is the fiction you continue to believe. To break out of it you have to want to. If you found it difficult to embody the two qualities I suggested, you might want to work more with them by doing a few explorations that allow you to get on the inside of the quality itself. For example, what color would you attribute to the quality? What is its tempo, its rhythm, its movement? Move in it in place. Take the shape of it. Make the sound of it. Take three steps forward in it. Two steps to the side. Give it life in these kinesthetic ways.

Then, try them on again as you did earlier and see if you can "play" them better. Am I asking you to be an actor when I say play them better? No. I am asking you to do consciously what you do in life every day when you express qualities you identify as "yours" or as "real" for you. You are playing those!

At the end of this chapter I will give you the nuts and bolts of a major assignment for this work of Act Two, The Museum Painting Experience. It will give you practice with concentration, with public solitude, and with becoming a new character whose qualities may enable you to awaken a next phase for your life.

## Scene Six
## *A Sense of Truth*

A story is told about French philosopher René Descartes. He was at a café and was asked if he would like a cup of coffee. He replied, "I think not" and he promptly disappeared.

You will recall that Descartes is famous for saying, "I think, therefore I am." Given that reality creation, you can see why he disappeared when he ceased thinking. For our purposes it might be better to say, "I am, therefore I think."

In life you convince yourself that truth is something that really exists, and that what you believe exists, really does. As with action on a stage, life is not what actually exists but that which can happen.

For example, in my early 20's I decided I would probably never marry. This was unusual back in the 1960's, but I had a nice life. I enjoyed dating multiple young men, had a good job, did well in school and didn't see why I would want to settle down with any one person. While I felt good about myself, I lacked love. I convinced myself that this lack really existed and began to feel emptiness.

At the time I was working for a man 23 years my senior who acted as a counselor for me. We enjoyed each other's company, shared deeply, and had warm feelings for each other. He was married and even if he had been single, he was chronologically too old for me. But life as it seemed to exist was not the reality I thought it was. I didn't know it, but he had fallen in love with me the first day I interviewed for the job, three years before.

Life is what can happen, not what appears to be real.

He told me of his love for me and it was as if a crack appeared in reality as I had known it. Suddenly I was aware of my deeper love feelings for him. The possibility of our forming a union grew before my eyes. I allowed myself to open to something I had never before considered. I began to imagine what life might be like if I were married to him and an entirely new reality and sense of truth was born.

I had previously convinced myself of a truth that had no place for a committed relationship. I believed that truth and, thus, it existed for me. The moment I moved from "this is what exists" to "this is what can happen," everything changed.

Your focus needs to be on your individual spirit and your knowing of its reality. The material world, which surrounds you like a stage set, supplies a general background for your feelings.

You dress life-energy in imagined circumstances and actions until your own sense of truth is satisfied and you have awakened your sensations.

Truth is actually whatever you sincerely believe. Truth and belief exist together. Without both of them co-existing, you would have difficulty living the part that you *think* you are playing.

From believing in the truth of one small action, you can feel yourself in your life role and have faith in the reality of the whole life-play. It is as simple as writing a letter to a family member far away and in that small act experiencing your place in the larger family.

In the case of the man I married, the one small action was responding to his proclamation of love. I let that in, opened in the whole of myself, allowed myself to feel my own love for him, and had faith that something wonderful could emerge. My whole life-play changed.

In the midst of your daily living you often go on drift. Your body is there but you are not. Your consciousness is elsewhere. This behavior interrupts your line of action, your line of purpose. This constitutes a break in the continuity of your life in consciousness. It causes blanks. These in turn become filled with thoughts and feelings, with private world ramblings that are extraneous to the life that you could be living in the clarity of the finer frequencies.

Consciousness is the awareness that you are playing yourself. When you cease to be conscious, you become the role (the character) and it plays you while you are out.

If you feel yourself drifting into unconsciousness, ask, what is my purpose? This will enable you to begin to direct your energy creatively.

## Act Two: How Am I? 87

Player functions only in energy. It is through physical action that Player brings the energy world into form. The more disciplined you are at honing your actions, the closer you come to giving congruous life to what is transpiring in the energy world.

The energy world is the unseen realm that is ever present; this is the realm of frequencies that Player registers in consciousness. From these frequencies the level of "actuality" (what can be seen) is brought into being through specific actions by the character.

What is even more important than the actions themselves is your presence while you embody them. Embodying leads to feeling and experience. **To experience is to know.** When you know, you have come full circle back to meet the energy world. When you think, you meet the private world, a far lesser experience.

The smallest physical movement fully expressed in given circumstances produces great feeling-experience. When you focus on what you have to do by way of an action, all the feelings underneath will surface.

Whenever you say something is real it is because you have conjured it up and invested yourself in it. Because you conjure up the reality you are equally free to release it.

Player is not some divine, perfect aspect of Self while the character is lesser, standing in the way of union. Player is the I AM, the one who registers frequencies and who creates the manifestation of those frequencies through character.

If, through character, you are functioning in a lesser way than you know yourself to be capable of, you cannot simply blame the character. You can't say, my character didn't do it right or fully enough. You can't because you are the very one who has creative jurisdiction over the character. If you are producing something lesser, it is an out-picturing of your own state of evolution. This is the best you as Player can achieve in this moment. You are seeing your own True Self in form. The form encourages the making of new choices and you are encouraged to register finer and finer frequencies and to align with those in your outer expression, through character.

There are many examples of people who lived the truth they registered and didn't settle for something lesser on the character level. They were committed to a purposeful life and they registered finer frequencies to support their purpose and to lead them to actions that were so potent they contributed to changing the world: Mahatma Gandhi, Mother Teresa, Martin Luther King, and Nelson Mandela, to name a few.

### *Exercise:*

You can practice in ways small and large. Is there a bit of unfinished business with someone in your life? Something you wanted to say but didn't? Give yourself the purpose of moving this energy in yourself and freeing it. Then give your character an objective. It might be to set healing in motion, or to build a bridge between you and the other, or to reawaken the relationship. This is the meaning your character will embody as you, Player, direct the action. You will call the other person, send forth love, build a bridge through softness and caring, and invite the other to respond. You will direct character to be open to receive and to be present to the flow between you with no expectations of what the outcome might be.

As you do this, observe your character expressions. Are you listening? Are you reaching out? Are you steady on the course of your chosen action and intention?

In this way you practice aligning your outer and inner selves.

## *Exercise:*

Now you can expand this to a larger step. Is there something else you might have done with your life if you had truly followed your inner calling? What interfered? What action can you choose now that would start you in the direction of recreating an earlier dream?

Remember that Player knows no limitations. If character begins to tell you that it is too late, or there is no opportunity, or it would require too much, hear all of this as a call to you, to the realm of consciousness where everything is possible. By holding a purpose and following through with actions, change can become a reality.

## Scene Seven
## *Units and Objectives*

A play on stage is divided into units. This makes it easier for actors to work with the subtle changes that occur from scene to scene, moment to moment. Your life can be approached in the same way; the units are signals that keep you functioning on a creative line. For each unit, you need to have an objective.

"Playing" objectives in life moments allows you to direct your energy consciously and fully. Objectives give meaning and purpose to your life and interactions.

An objective is "what do I want?" What do I want to create in this moment or unit?

**Objectives:**

- are always directed toward the person or situation with which you are directly involved
- should be personal and in tune with how you experience yourself
- should be creative
- should be alive and stimulating
- should be truthful

- should be attractive to you
- should be clear-cut and specific, not vague or general
- should have depth
- should be active, pushing you forward into creativity
- should always be active verbs; nouns call forth conceptual concepts whereas verbs call forth action and evoke feelings

Objectives allow you to do, to bring about change, to enliven the moment. They move your energy forward rather than seek results. Be interested in what you are doing and others will be interested in you.

When you are not functioning with an objective, when you have no specific purpose, you are not directing your life energy.

Objectives facilitate consciousness. I said this before but it is important to repeat: consciousness is the awareness that you are playing yourself. When you cease to be conscious, you become the role and it plays you while you are not aware.

It is important to enliven your actions with motivation, with objectives stemming from a larger purpose. The qualities you add as ingredients to your actions give vibrancy to them. When you are aligned with an objective you are truthfully performing life actions. When there is truth there is feeling and experience. Where there is feeling there is knowing.

For example, when I brought **The Theatre of Life** into being in 1981 I was motivated by an urge to reawaken my theatrical experience and training. I didn't want to return to professional acting, but I did want to find something to align with my life purpose which was to serve the creative process. I listened within to my intuition and my inner environment for becoming immediately lit up. I was directed to Stanislavski's books and I began to hear a joyful singing in my soul. I saw the possibility of encouraging others to use all the skills I knew to create their lives consciously. I had touched on a truth much larger than any I could have thought up in my mind. My feelings began to soar and as I brought each act into being my knowing unfolded like a rapidly opening flower.

Life is a circle. Everything originates in the energy world. It is the source. You, on Player level, register the frequency and manifest it through character action. You bring the energy into form by experiencing it. As you feel/experience the energy in specific action, you come to know. To know is to return to the energy world.

The essence of the entire work of **The Theatre of Life** is to live truthfully with a purpose. The sustaining of consciousness is enhanced tremendously by focusing on an objective. You hold everything intact by giving the character a specific to which to relate and on which to focus. The throughline from Player to character is unbreakable when you are focused on the objective.

## Exercise:

What is your life purpose for the current period of your life?

What are your major objectives?

What qualities can you activate through character to enhance your objectives?

How do your home environment and your work environment add to or detract from your becoming, from fulfilling your purpose and objectives, and from deepening your major relationships?

## The Major Experience for Act Two: The Museum/Painting Experience

*Note:* You may want to read all the way to the end of this chapter before beginning to do this exercise. The overview will help you be more conscious as you move through each step of the five or six days. Once you begin the experience, read the assignment for each day only without jumping ahead to the work you will do next.

**Day One:**

Make notes in answer to the following questions: What do you feel drawn to for the next phase of your life? How do you see yourself functioning, behaving? What do you see yourself doing?

Now, go to your local art museum. Take your digital camera if you have one and the notes you made.

At the museum, prepare yourself by going within, focusing on a center still-point in self. Enter the museum as a Player in Public Solitude. You are in the public place of the museum but you are in solitude within your creative self, investing your energy in the task at hand. You want to be conscious of self rather than self-conscious.

Ask yourself: What is burgeoning or emerging within me? What is calling to me from my inner self?

Your objective is to find a character in a painting that represents what is emerging or calling to you.

Begin a tour of the museum. Start with sculptures. Become the essence of the sculpture in shape, feeling, movement, etc. Recreate the sculptures with your own body and then register feelings, sensations, etc. (Remember to practice public solitude and to be conscious of self, not self-conscious.)

Following sufficient practice with this, go through the various galleries in the museum looking at paintings. You are looking for a specific painting. It is to have only one person in it. The person can be in any setting and anywhere in the setting. You are to allow the painting to draw you to its essence. It must call you. Its energy essence must draw you, whether or not it makes any sense to you. Settle on one painting. If it is a choice between two that are calling, check in the museum shop. If there is a print of one painting and not the other, you might want to choose the one with the print so that you can have it to work with. Or take a digital photo of the painting.

Having chosen one painting, spend 3 separate 15-minute intervals being with the essence of the painting. Do this in public solitude. Do this with concentration. You will spend the first 15-minute period just sitting, being with the painting, being in the essence of it.

**Take a Break**

Return to the painting, make notes of everything you see in the painting, all the details of background and what the figure looks like and is wearing, including colors, material, textures.

Then, for 15-minutes, assume the position you see in the painting and experience the essence of the figure and what it is to be this person in this scene. Merge with the essence of what you see.

**Take a Break**

For the third 15-minutes, assume the position of the character in the painting again, merging with the essence. Be conscious of what you experience.

Immediately upon return home from the museum, spend one more 15-minute period in the position of the person in the painting. Focus on merging with the essence of what you saw.

Review for yourself what you did to create an environment for becoming focused at the museum. How did you maintain your concentration? Were you distracted? How did you allow the distraction to occur?

In this first part of the exercise you were creating an inner environment for becoming by merging with the essence of the character in the painting.

**Day Two:**
Now you will embark on the second phase of the exercise. You will create an external environment so you can bring the character to life. Gather all the supplies you need to recreate the painting, and the character in the painting, in a place in your living environment. You will need materials for the background, including fabrics, makeup, the works.

Sit in front of the empty space where you will create the painting. Come to know it. Prepare in energy receptivity for your painting. Put your picture or print there and be present to it.

Using all the materials you have gathered, create the background of the painting, the environment in which your character will emerge.

Prepare the attire you will wear.

Clear the environment of any excess — what will not be used.

## Act Two: How Am I?

Lay out the character's garments in front of the painting environment you have created, carefully preparing them for the character who will emerge.

Prepare a small table a short distance away from the painting with a mirror and makeup you will need to make your face into the face of the character in the painting.

As you do all of the above, remind yourself that you are consciously creating an inner and outer environment for becoming.

**Day Three:**
*You might want to have a friend read the following instructions to you so that you can follow them while remaining involved in the creative process.*

Sit down at the makeup table. Place the reproduction or photo of the face in the painting in front of you. Look into the mirror. Allow yourself to see the molecules of the face reflected there. Move beyond seeing shape and form. Move into the essence of what you see in the painting. Bring that essence through these molecules and work with the substance of the face to make the substance take the shape of the essence in the painting. Feel the essence from the inside out, watching your face begin to become the essence.

## The Theatre of Life

Now begin to make up the essence, to apply makeup to your face so that you highlight the essence of what you are bringing forth. As Player you create it from within, and then you add the finishing touches to highlight, to shadow, to make the character look like what Player sees.

Finish the makeup and the hair. Clean up the make-up table.

Merge with the essence of the character until your body takes the shape of this character. Then, as this person, dress yourself in the clothes of this character.

Focus on the molecules of the being from the neck down. Go to where your character clothing lies. Allow yourself to become shapeless, formless. Allow your body to begin from the inside out to embody the essence of the painting figure and begin to dress. Your body and the attire will slowly emerge into the figure.

A new body will emerge into the clothing. You are filling the attire; it is not hanging on you. When you are fully formed, enter the painting and take the position of the character. Become the figure as you saw it and be frozen in time forever and ever.

Set a timer to go off after 10 minutes. When it does, make one single gesture within the painting.

This is a moment in time in your life. You are

sitting in this moment in time. Be present to yourself, to your environment, to everything in the larger room.

After making the single gesture, freeze again within the painting.

After a few moments, breathe out several times consciously, releasing the character you have created. As you remove the character's clothing, consciously experience letting this other being go and re-infusing yourself with your own qualities of being.

Remove the makeup, letting go of this other face you had embodied. Dress in your own character's clothing and fully reclaim your regular character self.

### Make Notes on the Following:
What is different/similar about the figure in the painting and your basic character? What changed in your body, in your thoughts, in your feelings, in your sensing? How did the environment of the painting facilitate what the figure was becoming? What is calling to the figure from within the painting? What is calling to you?

### Day Four:
The next day, continue with the experience. Note that when you take off your own character clothes, you take off the familiar essence you wear daily. If you want to create what you are becoming,

it is important for you to make conscious choices about the textures and fabrics you wear because they literally induce a personality. Make choices. Don't just put on an old self every day.

Return to your painting and sit in front of it, with the character's clothes in front of you. Recreate the face from the inside out, without make-up this time.

Close your eyes. Make your face a featureless mask. Release all tension. Create an empty shape waiting to come into being. Each time you exhale, breathe out through the formlessness, growing more shapeless with each exhale.

Beginning with the area of your mouth, feel the tingling energy there awaiting your creation of a mouth as you inhale. Bring into consciousness the essence of your painting's character. Breathe into that character and as you exhale this time, let the shape of the mouth in your painting begin to form itself on that space of your face. As you breathe in, become intimate with what is forming as a mouth. As you breathe out become conscious of how you hold your chin, your jaw, your teeth, and your tongue. It's all of one piece in this painting. It is a single expression frozen in time, of a mouth. A mouth caught in one second in time.

Now begin the same process on the breath with the cheeks, expanding out to the ears and feeling the bone structure coming into place. Stretch the flesh of the character across your cheeks.

In the center of your face is a throbbing of energy growing within, ready to protrude itself in shape as a nose, the nose of the character. Breathe out, allowing the nose to shape itself. Be present to the carving of the nostrils, the honing of the bone, the stretching of the skin.

Now, on the breath, feel eyebrows prickling out on the skin and taking shape. And there in the silent sound of the hollow beneath the eyebrows breathe out into the eyes that are taking form. They are under the lids, pushing, pushing, and pushing to the very first stirring of the lashes. Gently open to let the light in. Open slowly to see for first time. Look out through the eyes and see the small world around you.

Dress yourself as the character in the portrait, bringing the body into being as you put on articles of clothing.

Look into the painting. See it as a home created for you to live in for centuries. Take your place and position therein. Freeze in position.

Painted into the painting was the one thought or feeling of the moment of the one captured on canvas. See if you can touch that thought or feeling.

Being in touch with that thought or feeling, make one powerful gesture. Then return to the position in the painting.

Ask yourself, what happened the very moment before this moment in the painting? Why are you here? What is your purpose? Staying true to your purpose, make another gesture and then freeze in that position. One more single movement and freeze in that position.

As if you were in a slow motion movie, make a small series of movements staying true to your purpose. Move, freeze, move, freeze, etc.

Staying true to your purpose, if you could choose a position in which to be comfortable as this character, take that position and freeze.

At any point, allow to emerge organically a sound, a word, a phrase, something vocal. Remain true to your purpose as you do this. Hear your voice for the first time. Return to the original position and freeze.

Within the canvas, feel, let the thoughts flow, and speak to yourself aloud if that is there for you to do. Do not invent or impose anything. Allow everything to emerge organically, truthfully. Discover who you are.

Return to the frozen position. Begin to breathe out through your face, slowly releasing the features you have created. Release only your face, holding

## Act Two: How Am I? 103

your body in position. Create formlessness in your face. Then reconstruct your own character's face in the formlessness. Let your own face be new and fresh, tingling with life.

Breathe the character out of your body. Let the removal of garments help in the release of the character. When you put on your own garments, recreate your own character in the process.

**Take Time to Reflect and Make Notes:**
Were you stronger in the creation process today? What was most exciting or disturbing to you? What do you know about this character thus far that you didn't know when you first met? What is this character's purpose as you saw it today? What do you know about yourself today that is new?

Let go of all the character's clothing except for one key piece that awakens the whole essence of the character.

Write a paragraph beginning with "I," describing yourself with the qualities you have seen in the character in the painting.

**Day Five:**
On a subsequent day, take your notebook to your painting. Sitting or standing in front of your painting, direct yourself in the process of releasing your own familiar characteristics and moving into a formless state.

Stand up in the ready state. Take up into your hands the garment you have chosen. Breathe in the essence of this character. Let the character's face and essence emerge in you. Move around in place in the garment.

Move into the painting and take the position that was painted. Be aware that this is a unit. It is one small unit of life caught and held on a canvas.

Focus on your objective right now. What do you want in this very moment? How can you get what you want? Bring your painting to life. What qualities do you need to embody to support you in walking about, moving about in your own canvas, in public solitude? As the character in the painting, speak to yourself aloud about what you want and how you can get it.

**Day Six:**
Return to the painting and take your position therein.

What are your predominant qualities that make you different, physically and in personality? Settle in on two or three and breathe life into them as you sit there in the moment.

What is your objective right in this moment? What is it you want? In your canvas, give full life to these qualities. Get up and move about in them and explore out loud what you want and how you can get it.

Resume the painted position. Look at yourself through the eye of your inner observer. See the character in the painting. See your own character simultaneously. What is the same in both? What is true of both characters? What more is the character in the painting calling you to do? What does the character in the painting call forth from you?

Take a moment to say goodbye to the character in the painting, to say thank you for being. Breathe this character out, loosening it from face and body, removing garments as you are ready. Bring back to yourself the characteristics of your own character and those from the character in the painting that you now want.

## *For Conscious Review:*

How did the painter create an environment for becoming for the figure? What colors, textures, and content did the painter use?

What was the character saying to you? What was calling to you? What qualities do you want to express?

What is your most important learning from the painting experience and about yourself in it?

**106   The Theatre of Life**

## Creating a Character in a Painting

Below are some examples of characters created during "live" **Theatre of Life** sessions. On the left, putting on makeup and hair pieces while looking at the face in the painting. On the right, taking their positions in the paintings as the character.

Linda Luster.

Carolyn Hudson.

### Act Two: How Am I?   107

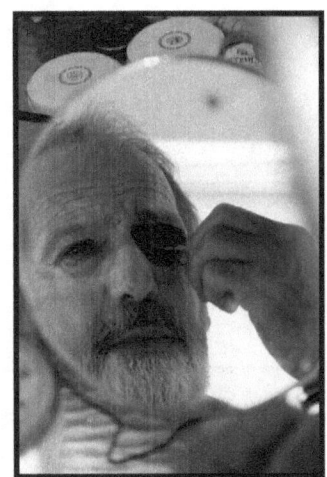

**Herman Warsh** causes a character to emerge, full blown.

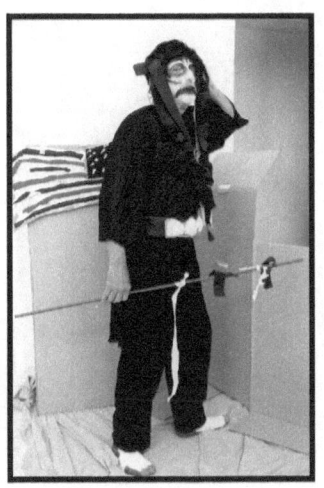

## 108   The Theatre of Life

Above, **Jane Nichols** makes up her face while looking at the portrait and then becomes the character in her environment. Below, **Esther Bell** expresses the feelings of the character she is portraying.

## Act Two: How Am I? 109

*Below, left,* **Fernand Villemure** *creates a woman character.*
*Below, right,* **Shirley Routliffe** *creates a man character.*

*Below, left,* **Suzanne Himmelwright** *and right,* **Linda Reisser** *created environments for characters from paintings and then embodied the characters within their environments.*

## Time for Reflection:
Having completed Act Two, take time as Player to reflect on your own inner and outer environments for becoming. Are there any changes you now see that you want to make?

# ACT THREE

# What Am I?

"I learned we do not *have* feelings. We *create* feelings. We do not have to take on the feelings of others."
— *James Stavoy, San Francisco, CA*

"Strength lies in expressing feelings consciously: to go through the feelings and not stay in them; to not be afraid of feelings or deny them. Feelings happen *through* the character, not *to* the character. All possible feelings are available to me."
—*Diana Farquharson, Belleville, ON*

"Keeping in mind 'What do I want?' helps the expression of my feelings be congruent with my life in the moment."
— *Esther Bell, Ashland, OR*

"If I give myself time to feel and not react, I can see to create artistically. I can give shape and form to what I see within. It is a solemn occasion to know that your world is created by you."
— *Eleanor Arnau, San Diego, CA*

"I experienced the energy that comes before I choose a feeling, and I have experienced my ability to express feelings consciously so that they serve my purpose."
— *Andy Gould, Flagstaff, AZ*

"I have the ability to harness my feelings. I can breathe into my solar plexus when I have a feeling and see where the energy takes me. When I clearly direct my feelings I can use them as effective tools to play out my purpose and objective in daily life, rather than allowing them to trap me."
— *Elizabeth Day Bradley-Howard, San Francisco, CA*

"I learned to loosen the screws, to trust the spontaneous expression of my feelings, to encourage creative feelings and let them guide me, and to move physically in a spontaneous way."
— *Jerry Howard, Waltham, MA*

"If I was afraid of feelings before, I'm not anymore. They are much easier to register and express if I truly breathe into my whole being and take time to be totally present to myself and my environment."
— *Bette Myerson, Taos, NM*

## Scene One
## *How Player Experiences Itself*

What am I? I am the consciousness that experiences myself as I interact in the world.

I experience myself as Player through the character or personality. The character is the vehicle for transporting the Power-to-be-Conscious into form or functionality. The character is a configuration of units of energy that serves to manifest what Player registers in the energy world.

The primary and most active way of experiencing self is through feelings. The mode of thinking, analyzing, conjecturing, or measuring is far inferior. It provides you with an assessment rather than an experience. The mind can organize for you but it cannot know. Knowing comes of feeling.

*Exercise:*
Try a little experiment to see how willing you are to feel, to experience. **Record** the following words so that you can play them for yourself as you are ready for the next and the next. The words are **joy, guilt, outrage, suffering, tenderness, anger, and uproarious laughter.**

Now, sit with your eyes closed and the recorder at your side. Play the first word and stop the recorder. Quickly allow your mind to immediately recall a time in your life when you experienced this feeling.

As soon as you touch the experience immerse yourself in it, remembering the event, the people present, what happened, the sights, smells and colors, etc. The mind serves us in remembering all of this.

Now move from the memory to the feelings you felt at the time and, with your eyes closed, give them expression in sound or even movement. Feel the feelings again, right now.

Then go to the next key word and the next.

Each time you activate your feelings you are awakening the solar plexus, the energy center that corresponds to your digestive system, your "gut." To function powerfully in relation to feelings, you need to direct your life force *out through* the solar plexus not *into* the solar plexus.

The word "feelings" is a label for a frequency band of energy. Specific feelings are Player's designed expressions of heretofore unconfigurated energy. You have a choice about the shape you give to the feeling energy you are experiencing. Player registers and expresses through character. You don't *have* feelings. You *create* them.

For example: Someone shouts loudly at you. You experience energy movement in the solar plexus. That energy, as yet, has no label, no form. It cannot be identified as a specific feeling, only as

## Act Three: What Am I? 115

feeling. You might respond by creating fear, or anger, or tenderness. You choose the shape to give the intensity of energy you are registering.

Your creation of a specific feeling, expressed through character, is now recorded in your character-expression repertoire. When you, Player, are functioning *unconsciously* through character, the fear or anger or tenderness is readily available to present itself as a response to a similar circumstance, even when inappropriate. You might well suffer what is known as unfounded fear, anger, tenderness, because your response came from the memory or a previous shout and was not really appropriate to the now moment.

When you look back consciously to a time of expressed feeling and see that the feeling has changed, you are able to appreciate the power of time. Time transmutes. It is a sculptor, making a gallery piece of an expression that can be visited in the museum of the mind at any time. These are now your emotional memories.

### *Exercise:*

As you proceed with this feeling exploration, do some reflection at the end of the day. How did you empower and/or dis-empower yourself during the day by expressing your feelings or repressing them? Also, recall a feeling you were conscious of during the day. How did you express it? What were you satisfied with or dissatisfied with in the expression?

## Scene Two
## *Feelings vs. Emotions*

Just as visual memory serves you by calling up forgotten places, events, and persons, and sends them as images across your inner screen, emotional recall serves to recreate feelings already experienced. A key word, a smell, an object, can bring the feelings back full force, as you have seen. Sometimes the relived feelings are as strong, stronger, or sometimes weaker. They are as strong because you have reentered the event as it was, or because you haven't let go of any of it. They can be stronger because you now feel freer to express what wasn't expressed then. Or they can be weaker because you called up more energy than you needed at the actual time of the event, or because you have now released the intensity of what you had been holding.

Sometimes, a completely contrary feeling presents itself in place of what had been experienced or expressed. This may be the truer feeling that was under the surface but you couldn't touch at the time or wouldn't allow to appear. You might really have been feeling wounded, for example, but you expressed irritation instead.

Your physical senses enable you to touch into

## Act Three: What Am I? 117

the emotion-sensor apparatus. Your artistic intuition, your Player consciousness, allows you to direct your awareness. In those moments, specific feelings are on the verge of being created.

Feelings are general sensations or frequencies registered by Player through the solar plexus chakra and then configurated into a specific expression. Because feelings are energy frequencies, they move quickly and so do their expressions.

Emotions are particular expressions through the character that have been sustained past the moment, often too long past the moment.

We sometimes get stuck in the specific because we become identified with it and enamored of it. We then live in patterned versions of ourselves. The good thing about this is that we create careers for psychologists.

A helpful thing to do is to move the energy that is bottled in emotions, to allow that energy to be reshaped by you. One way to have an experience of that is to work with clay. (It would be helpful to have another person, a partner, do this experience with you.)

### *Exercise:*

Go out to a store and buy some molding clay. Spread out a newspaper and place a chunk of the clay in front of you. Recall a time of great distress (pain, anger, fear, etc.). Reenter the memory: its circumstances and the senses and feelings associated with it. In your own inner self, retell the event to yourself in silence and re-feel the feelings.

Using the clay, mold the memory into the shape as you experienced the event then.

Bring your creation to your partner. Tell the partner about the event from the now perspective, recalling feelings, but letting them be mixed with now. If your partner also molded an experience, let the partner report as well.

When each of you has shared, or when you have shared, remodel the clay so that it is more representative of the sharing about the event that you just did with your partner.

Describe for your partner the transmutation of the energy as you experienced it. Let your partner do the same.

Then bring the energy to life in your body by making your body into the shape of the first sculpture and then moving it through the transmutation process and into the second/current sculpted stage.

When you and your partner have done this and given each other feedback, sit down with the clay one more time and re-sculpt it so that the memory takes a shape still further harmonious with how you currently experience the integration of the memory.

Share with your partner the changes you experienced. If the feelings changed, identify from what to what.

## *Make Some Notes:*

What did you discover about yourself in relation to feelings and activating/expressing them?

What surprised you most in recalling the memory or in the execution of the expression, or in the transmutation?

## Act Three: What Am I?

Did you allow sufficient feeling energy to surface in memory, in clay, in partner sharing, in body?
Did you hold back?

This kind of examination will enable you to more consciously deal with feelings and emotions as your inner growth progresses.

Make a commitment to breaking patterns, both emotional and outer behavioral patterns. For example, tonight eat dinner with your primary hand only.

## Scene Three
## Empowering Self Through Recall

Feelings come spontaneously and they are also stored as memories. Spontaneous feelings are easier to change than memories. However you are not always conscious that you are actually creating spontaneous feelings. They just happen and they affect you. If you are present as life is happening, you can create the spontaneous feelings (that is, give them a particular name) and choose an expression for them.

The recalling, reliving, and redoing of memories is a way to practice empowering yourself to be present to the moment prior to a feeling creation. Sometimes you have trouble allowing yourself to feel something. Grief is a good example because it is so painful. Anger is another because you may have been taught to hide "not nice" feelings.

A way to give yourself permission to express a particular feeling is to come at the feeling you can't express through a back door, the door of previous memories. You can remember a time when you were sad about the death of a pet or when you were angry with a childhood friend. By reentering that memory you awaken similar feelings. Once the

## Act Three: What Am I?

feelings are activated, you can gently move yourself into the current grief or jump into the current anger and let the feelings flow.

Your character is your basic vehicle of expression – the expression of the "I AM" through the personality. You respond to life events and you create feelings that appear appropriate for the moment. Those feelings are expressions of Player through character. They are not determined by the event, though when you are unconscious, they seem to be.

An actor must never lose self on stage. She must always be an artist creating what she is enacting. The moment she loses self, loses her awareness that she is creating artistically, she departs from living her role and moves into exaggerated, overplayed or dull acting – or no acting at all because the role has her!

In life, overplaying or being melodramatic is like pulling at the "heartstrings" and the "emotional udders" at the same time and overdoing both until you and others are exhausted and drained.

If you do not stay true to who you are, if you are not centered in yourself as Player, you slip over into a character facsimile that responds unconsciously and is caught in its own illusion of itself.

Player is the one who can play anything. Player creates anything and gives it life as/through character.

The key in relation to feelings is to know that you, Player, are the only one shaping and creating specific expressions through character and that the entire gamut is open to you – not just the primary responses to which character has grown accustomed.

To facilitate your coming to know this fully so that feeling-expressions will not so easily manifest unconsciously, it is good to practice the re-creation of feelings at will, deciding on what to feel and creating that feeling as fully as you wish.

The actor does this constantly when playing roles that call for his expression of feelings and his recreation of the same ones night after night. We, life-actors, do this constantly too, but we need to know that we are doing it consciously so that we are free to make choices.

For example, if someone is nagging you, wanting more than you are willing to give in that moment, make a choice about what feeling to create and express. If you are functioning unconsciously and not making a choice, irritation or annoyance might jump right in. If, on the other hand, you decide to touch tenderness in yourself and to give it expression, your response to the one who is nagging will be very different. Rather than trying to brush the person away like a disturbing fly, you will say a few kind words and tell the person you are busy at the moment and cannot give what is being requested. The person will likely feel met, even by this small gesture, and stop nagging. You didn't automatically feel tenderness; you chose to give it shape and form.

## Act Three: What Am I?

The inner qualities/characteristics you have stored in your Emotional Recall Bank qualify you to automatically "play" some roles and not others. For example, if you have memories of being aggressive, bullying, and loud as a child, you can easily call on that behavior in adulthood. If you were painfully shy or felt the despair of not being able to stand up for yourself, you might not be able to automatically move into aggressive or loud behavior.

When you move from functioning automatically to functioning consciously, your Emotional Recall Bank can be a resource for supplementing the feelings you choose to express and you will not be ruled by how you used to be. You can have preferences but you need not be ruled by them.

Similarly, when you function consciously you are not bound by any given personality expression. How is it that you can express widely different personalities? You can because Player is not any of them. No particular characteristic belongs to Player. The seed of all qualities, all feelings, all expressions is there for Player to develop.

Rather than identifying with any one way of being and saying "this is my nature," your true nature is the natural movement from Player through character utilizing all the life elements that are available. In this way, what character expresses is what Player is registering.

## Exercise:

Here is an experience for working with memories, registering the accompanying feelings, and choosing which feeling to bring to life. In this experience you will offer yourself images I have provided for you and you will allow to awaken in you whatever the memory evokes from your own life. *Allow* is the key word. Don't look for a feeling — feel. Respond to the impetus and let it take you, then guide and direct it. Feelings are not to be gotten rid of. Feelings are to be used to take in information about your own experience and what you know. Feelings are to be used to empower expression.

Place the book in front of you, open to this page, turning the page as you need to. Sit comfortably in a chair with your eyes closed. Breathe deeply and relax, opening your eyes when you need to move to the next instruction.

One at a time, offer yourself these images and journey to your own memory and to the accompanying feelings. Feel the feelings. When you finish with each, move to the next. You set the pace.

> The sight of a small child holding a parent's hand
>
> The smell of a musty trunk
>
> The taste of ice-cold watermelon
>
> The sound of a train in the distance

The touch of stubble on a man's face

The sight of adults fighting and arguing

The smell of soft summer rain

The taste of hot cereal

The sound of a creaking door

The touch of wet wind on your face

The sight of new buds in the spring

The smell of a rose

The taste of a hotdog with mustard
    and sauerkraut

The touch of warm soft skin
    in the early morning

The sight of a circus

The smell of hot chocolate

The taste of cold milk and cookies

The sound of a muffled voice
    in the other room

The feel of mud beneath your feet

The sight of a funeral

The smell of baby powder

The taste of cotton candy

The sound of a clock ticking

The feel of wool on your body

Be aware of how many memories and feelings came to life in you through this sensory recall.

Choose one particular memory that was awakened in you. Recall the sensory stimulus that awakened the memory and its feelings. Staying connected with the senses, tell yourself this experience out loud, describing what you saw, heard, smelled, touched, and tasted, allowing the feelings to flow as they come.

Next, leave the senses aside and talk aloud about the facts of the event as they occurred. Observe the difference. I suspect you will see that you created much more feeling by tuning into the senses than you did by going into your head and retelling the facts.

## *Make Some Notes In Your Journal:*

Take a few moments to reflect on how you might have related to feelings in the past and, as a result of the above brief exercise, how your ability to activate and express feelings has changed.

## Scene Four
# Enhancing Feeling Expression Through Outer Stimuli

Surroundings tremendously influence your feelings. That is why it is important to pay attention to your environment and to be sure it supports your emergence as a creative life-artist. Externals are stimuli to your capacity to feel and to experience. You come to know yourself as the Self who registers frequencies and expresses them through the experiences of your character as you relate to outer stimuli.

Player is larger, not smaller, than any feeling. No feeling is large enough to have power over you. You have the power, not the feeling. The feeling renders you powerful by fueling your awareness and creativity.

Expressing feelings is not releasing and letting go of them. It is discovering them, giving life to them through expression, and experiencing them. This is to let them move you into action, not into dissipation of the energy or abandonment of the feeling.

There are styles of family behavior in relation to feelings. You learned as you were growing up in what situations it was appropriate to have and to express feelings, and you were to do it as your elders did. You may have had fear of having feelings because of the power in them and how that power affected the self who was having the feeling and others who were in the presence of it.

You may have been told to stifle your feelings or to control them. Seeking to control (anything) is the greatest illusion from which egos suffer. If you manage to have any semblance of control, what you are really doing is restricting energy. This represents lack of power.

Letting go of control doesn't have to lead to floundering, or weakness, or pacifying self with addictions. To let go of control can be replaced by going forth from the center of self with power, going forth creatively into the unknown to meet what is coming. Be present and deal with life as you meet it, not in advance. This is to function fully in the powerful now moment. Rather than being in control, you are in communion with what you are confronting.

Every memory of then can be infused with new feelings by bringing them from then to now. For example, you experienced anxiety during your first childbirth; you might now bring a feeling of great joy to the memory, the joy that emerged when the infant was delivered. Now you can have the experience of the joy that was there under the anxiety. In this example you can see that during the initial childbirth the inner and outer environments influenced the feelings you were having. Now those environments are different. Hence, you can infuse the memory of that experience with new feelings, feelings that may have been under the surface back then but were suppressed by the anxiety.

Another way of practicing with creating and expressing feelings is by allowing yourself to shift a feeling right in the midst of expressing one. For example, you and a friend are caught in a disagreement. You are both unwilling to give in but neither of you wants to continue in the nonproductive stalemate. Take a deep breath, relax your furrowed brow, and introduce laughter. Laugh right out loud and say, "I can't believe we are doing this! Let's quit." You have shifted the focus and the energy. You have instantly created a new environment. Both of you can now laugh, let go, and move on. Through practicing shifting of feelings, you open yourself to a wider range of expression.

## *Exercise:*

What are you feeling right now? Take the time to breathe into your solar plexus to register the energy and to give it a specific shape using your body.

Choose and embody an antithetical physical position, something that doesn't at all express what you were just feeling. What happens to the feeling? How has it changed?

This is a quick way to see the effect of outer stimuli. The body position changes and so does the feeling, often in surprising ways.

Continue by using your imagination to put yourself in an environment from your past. For example, return to a memorial service for a loved one. Step into the primary feeling you were experiencing then. Let's say it was deep sadness. Feel the sadness but allow your memory to shift to a time when you and the deceased were enjoying a happy moment together. Note that you have changed both the feeling and the outer stimulant.

Now, take the feeling from the happy time and bring it into the memorial service and into your sadness. Doing this may well contribute to a lessening of grief and the replacement of that grief with gratitude for the loved one and for the privilege you had of knowing and loving this person.

Choose a few different environments from memory to recreate and bring the same feeling of happiness or gladness into those, observing what happens to the feeling, or to the memory.

In this exercise you are not trying to eliminate what you once felt. Instead, you are experiencing how the creation of a new environment can affect and even change feelings. Your goal is to have direct experience with your creation of feelings, what enables you to create them, and what facilitates your ability to change them at will.

### *Exercise:*

Another approach would be to create a small environment and see what you feel as you do it. For example, gather up some of your favorite things: a piece of jewelry, a small teddy bear, a baseball, a scarf, a hat, a sweater, etc. Set these items up on

## Act Three: What Am I?

a table, creating a small tableau, and sit in front of them. Check on what you are feeling as you now sit before that created environment. Leave your area while retaining the feeling and sit in another room which is a completely different environment and does not contain a collection of your favorite things. Try to maintain your feeling. Then allow the feeling to shift as it is affected by the current environment.

## Scene Five
## *Living in the Now Moment*

Most characters live lives of repetition. We encounter a stimulus and bring to it an old response, perhaps because it requires less energy than taking things in fresh and choosing a now response.

For example, there are people in our lives whom we judge on the basis of previous experiences with them. They did whatever they did and we don't like them because of what they did. The next time we meet up with them, we still don't like them because of the past and because we are too lazy or stuck to meet them as if for the first time. If we lived in the moment, we might discover many things we like about them.

Sometimes we relive past events each time we are in similar circumstances. For example, if we were once frightened by the darkness or being home alone at night, we might continue to experience that fear for a lifetime. One way to break such a pattern is to give ourselves new data with which to work each time we are alone at night. The new data can take many forms: "I am alone and I am safe. Nothing is happening to cause me to be afraid." Or, "I am a strong and capable adult. I have many options, including calling family or friends if I am concerned, or even 911." Slowly you would

## Act Three: What Am I? 133

begin to build a new relationship with darkness and aloneness.

The key in relation to previously held convictions which intervene uninvited, and to past events which evoke the same old feeling in a similar circumstance, is to be present to the now moment, to the current conditions and what they are evoking from us. We need to go beyond the emotional memory of the character which is very limited and boxes us into old familiar feelings. In contrast, in the emotional womb of Player all the feeling possibilities reside and we get to select which to bring to life. This opens a whole world of choices to us.

The more you enter Player's emotional womb, the richer your creativity will be in each moment. Spontaneous feeling, fully expressed, gives vitality to the purpose and objectives you hold.

There are other ways previous experiences can serve you. As with many people, you may have strong feeling responses to memories of past events. It's almost as if the old memories and feelings are ghosts. They move into your field. Player registers the energy, and character unconsciously jumps in and begins reliving the old response as if the circumstance were happening here and now to you. You think you are feeling what you are feeling!

The previous experience can serve as a reality check. A good way to determine whether a feeling from the past is actually alive today is to recall an emotional memory and re-enter it.

While you are descending into a previous memory, it is the you of today who is doing the remembering and you may be inviting yourself to have a new view. By remaining in the now moment you will bring the past and present together in a new way.

## *Exercises:*

1. Choose an event in the past of your character's life which was highly charged emotionally, when you felt or expressed great feeling, five years ago or more. Suggestions include anger, sadness, joy, grief, thrill, shock, fear, outrage, and despair.

Sit quietly in a chair and talk out loud, first about the environment in which the event took place, recounting the smells, the colors, the visual, the tastes, and the kinesthetic dimensions before entering into the actual event itself. There will come a moment of shifting, or immersion in the event. Allow yourself to fully experience the feelings. As you do, see if they are the same as when the event occurred? Or, are they stronger or weaker, or perhaps completely different?

2. For practice in being aware of spontaneous feelings that arise in you and for practice in choosing which ones you wish to bring to life, open the phone book and, at random, call three local strangers and ask for their restaurant suggestions. Tell them you are new in town and you thought this would be a great way to discover good places to eat. Be aware of the feeling responses you get from those on the phone. It will likely range from friendly and helpful to suspicious or rude. Observe your own feelings in response to theirs and the choices you make.

# Scene Six
# Communion

It is possible to look at things or people and to really see them, but it is also possible to look and not see. If you look at something or at another strictly through your private world view (your character's eyes), you might see only what fits with your past experience and not what is actually in front of you. If you look and *really* see in the moment, you will have a new experience in which you learn something about yourself and/or about the other.

Whether present in the now moment or functioning through the limitations of your private world, you are constantly interacting with situations, things and people, and the most satisfactory interaction is when you are in communion, giving and receiving, living in a spiritual intercourse.

## *Exercise:*

Try this for yourself. With whom or with what are you in communion at this moment? By communion I mean, what are you sensing, or feeling, or with what are you merging? Close your eyes and ears, be silent, and see if you can find a single second when you are not in contact with something, someone, some part of yourself, or some frequency.

### *Exercise:*

We most often use a mirror to see how we look. Stand in front of a mirror and use it instead *to see*, to see the real you. Look in the mirror asking, "What am I?" Am I a congruent expression of what I am experiencing?

Speak aloud to self. What do you see as you look at yourself?

Breathe into your solar plexus, creating feelings, and let the sharing of them emerge in your facial expressions. Tell yourself aloud what you see.

Use the following three pages of facial expressions. Recreate these in the mirror. Recreate the feelings that evoked the face. Throughout this practice, allow your face to be mobile and retain communion with your own self.*

*The source of these drawings is unknown.

## Act Three: What Am I?   137

# 138  *The Theatre of Life*

## Act Three: What Am I?

## 140   The Theatre of Life

*The workshop participants below were using the faces offered on pages 137-139 above to practice expressing feelings in their own faces. We offer their examples to inspire you.*

**Andy Gould,** *above.*
**Diana Farquharson,** *below.*

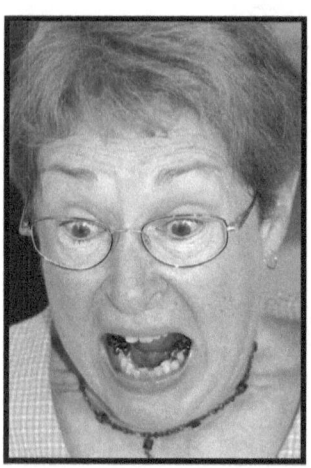
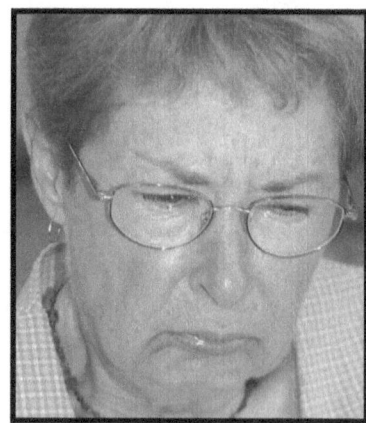

## Act Three: What Am I?  141

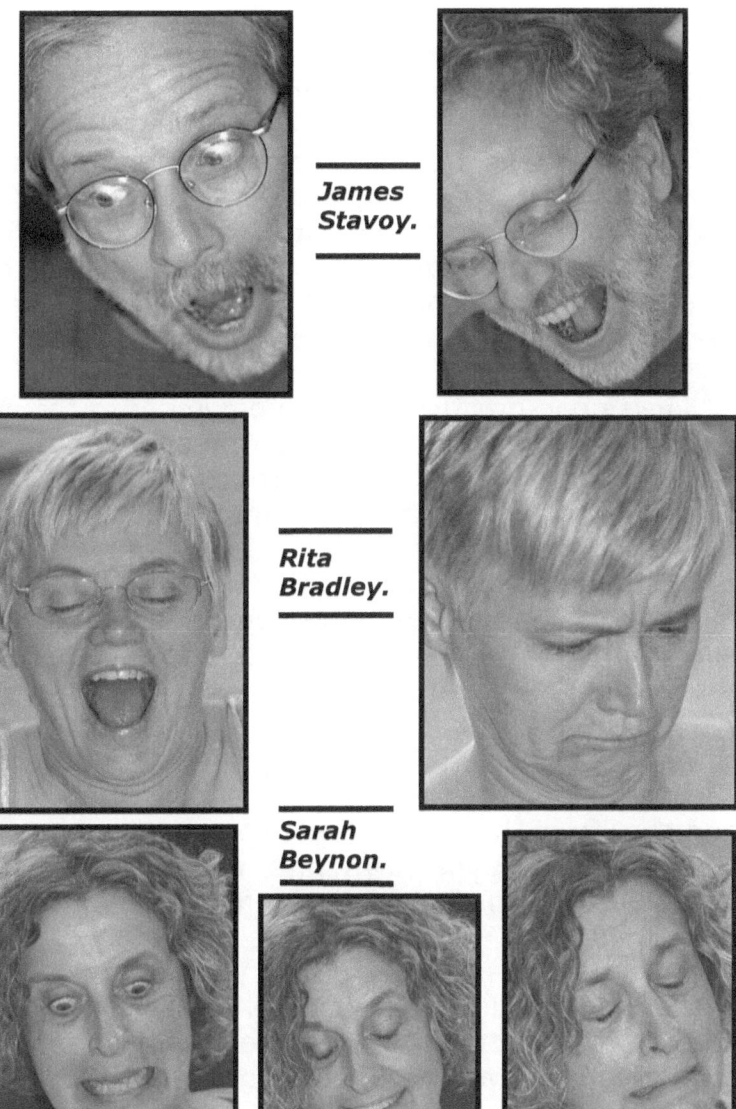

James Stavoy.

Rita Bradley.

Sarah Beynon.

As you complete this scene, take some time to reflect on responses to this sentence: I communicate with myself most effectively and directly by ... when...

*For example:* I communicate with myself most effectively and directly by speaking honestly when I would rather fool myself. Or, I communicate with myself most effectively and directly by using the most descriptive words possible when I want to experience something on the feeling level.

It is good practice and reinforcement to remind yourself of what you do well or effectively, and to remind yourself how you do that. The more you bring the "what" and the "how" into your awareness the stronger both become.

Internal dialogs such as this allow you to commune with yourself, to value your inner assets, to align with what you know, and to boost your self-esteem.

Direct communication with another which includes listening, hearing, really seeing, receiving, and responding, leads to enhancement of your life and the life of the other. Direct communication with yourself leads to your own inner and outer growth; it enables you to maintain your focus on your purpose in life.

When you can relate fully to yourself exercising creative jurisdiction over your feelings and thoughts, you will have better and richer communication with others and you will be able to consciously encourage that.

## Act Three: What Am I?

In my work as a personal consciousness coach I often work with people who divert their eyes or dodge answers to questions when they feel uncomfortable or don't know how to respond. Because I fully relate to myself, I do the same with persons I am coaching. I hold my eyes on them without wavering so that when they return from their own diversions they find me right there, ready to meet them and to encourage them to respond, to find a response within themselves. Because I have established jurisdiction over my own feelings and thoughts, I am able to guide them into and through their own feelings. I am unafraid of whatever they might touch and this gives them permission to go deeper and to reveal to themselves what is calling.

Too often people choose superficial conversation with others. When they do, everyone involved leaves unsatisfied. What a waste. Our time with each other is precious and if it is substantive, it benefits all of us because we will have added meaning to the whole of human interaction.

What Am I? I am the energetic expression of human evolution. Through my actions, my presence, and my willingness to commune meaningfully with all of life I contribute to the transformation of energy occurring through each of us and in all of us.

## Scene Seven
## *Sustaining Conscious Communion*

When you play your character consciously, you have the ability to stay present in each moment and to each person with whom you are relating in the life-play. When you become distracted from knowing self as Player, you can fall under the sway of your own personal life and its dramas. In these lapses, you are transported out of the now moment and its power, out of a light-filled mode, into self-consciousness where your private world takes over. This causes you to live in *pre*formed patterns rather than performance-in-the-now through Player's creational power. When these lapses are frequent, they ruin the continuity of the life-role you are developing and they break your communication with others.

Constantly breaking the line of communication distorts or kills the conscious expression of Player registry.

No playwright would present his characters in a state of unconsciousness or sleep, or without some active inner life. The audience would be as turned off as the characters on the stage. Yet, we

## Act Three: What Am I?   145

sometimes function that way in daily life. Or imagine a play where no characters talk to each other or where they refrain from interacting with each other. The audience would be utterly bored. In our life plays we often fail to communicate with the other characters in our scenes.

Communion is our mode of merging with each other in a conscious union as one being. And that communion with each other is the outer mirror of the inner communion between Player and the One.

The film *Ordinary People* provides a perfect example of communication and the lack thereof. I would urge you to watch it to see the effort that is required for remaining in communion and also how easy it is to slip into one's private world and get lost in there.

A useful practice is to purposely allow yourself to go on drift in the midst of an interaction with another and to observe where the distraction takes you and how you need to gather your awareness to bring yourself fully back into the exchange. If you can consciously remove yourself, you can much more easily choose consciously to stay connected.

## *Exercise:*

Try this. Make a phone call to a person you have not talked with in over 20 years to express your gratitude for how they empacted your life. You want to establish communion not only with the other but also with this period of your life and you in it. Observe how alive you become and how much of yourself you bring to the interaction.

We are advanced and enlightened regarding what we don't want in our lives, but we are often not as clear about what we do want and how to make that a reality. This is another reason we need to communicate with ourselves directly and clearly. Then, once we identify what we want, we need to give it expression through our actions and intentions.

## *Exercise:*

Observe yourself as you engage with other persons in your life. How expressive are you? Do you use the whole of yourself to express? Is your way of speaking filled with different intonations or is your delivery flat and dull? The more animated you are, the more life-force you bring to the reality you wish to create.

Do you stay visually and emotionally connected with others when you share a scene? Evaluate your ability to sustain conscious communion with others.

## Scene Eight
## *Communion with Self*

Truly communing with another requires conscious presence and unblocked receptivity. Characters often replace real communication with ordinary imitations of it. They *seem* to be there rather than actually being there. This is easiest to understand when character is simply being phony in an exchange. What I'm talking about is larger than that.

For example, when caring is expressed toward you, your character's attachments and private world thoughts can be barriers to direct communion. This limits spontaneous caring and expression.

Let's say you had a few bad experiences with people you trusted. As a result, you became overly cautious when people were nice to you. Along comes a new person in your life who is attentive, friendly, and wants to give to you. The person expresses caring, but instead of receiving the offering, you pull back. You are not as open as you might be. You cling to your character's attachment to self-protection and you reawaken thoughts that tell you to beware because you might get hurt.

If you choose your private world over full interaction with this person you may well miss out on a nourishing and completely safe relationship.

When, instead, Player awareness is present, character becomes a servant of Player and can receive the full expression of caring without interference.

Feeling is the mother of expression. Expression is communing with others through self. This is fueled by knowing what you seek to express, how much feeling energy you wish to bring to it, and what your objective is. When you know what you want to communicate you are then able to direct your energy flow consciously. You discover more of what you are feeling as you express it, because Player observes character as it is performing in the world.

## *Exercise:*

Take a look at your own character. Name a character mode of expression that empowers and one that disempowers you, and how this is true.

*For example:* A mode of expression that empowers me is establishing firm eye contact. A mode of expression that disempowers me is when I too quickly touch and express feelings, especially when I have not consciously created them. Another mode of expression that empowers me is speaking in a clear, well-projected voice when I am addressing someone. One that disempowers me is trying to control a situation.

Name a spontaneously intuitive expression through character from the past that surprised you greatly when you did it and perhaps still does when

### Act Three: What Am I? 149

you think of it. How did it affect you then? How could you use it to advantage now?

Now, I invite you to practice embodying expression, one step removed, through the use of a monologue. If you have play scripts at home, flip through to find a powerful speech that was delivered by a character in the play. You can also use a Shakespearean soliloquy or a good size speech by a character in a novel.

The writer of the play or novel has written the words and developed a character through whom to express. You will embody this character and practice being a servant of Player by playing an objective, expressing feelings and embodying helpful qualities.

## *How to Work on a Monologue*

- Read it silently to yourself a few times.
- Read it aloud, without overlay of expression.
- Read it aloud with expression that is organic to the words and what drew you to them. What are the major feelings to be expressed?
- Determine the overall objective of the speech and focus on it throughout.
- Determine the dominant qualities in the character of this monologue and activate them in yourself.

- Create a small environment in which to perform the monologue later for family or a friend.
- Read aloud, script in hand and up on your feet, awakening feeling.
- Stage it, by which I mean, decide when and where you want to move as you speak the lines of dialog.
- Rehearse: focus on playing the objective, enhancing it through qualities and expressing it through feeling.
- When finished, make a brief note of how you empowered and disempowered yourself as you rehearsed.

Once you feel comfortable with what you have prepared, invite others in and "perform" it for them. This doesn't mean "act it out." It means make the words and the character your own by creating and activating the feelings and embodying them.

Receive feedback from the "audience" and then evaluate your own work.

## *Reflections:*

What were your discoveries about "performing?"
What empowered and disempowered you?
What can serve you now in self-communion?
What did you notice about the role of the director and about the importance of the directorial func-

### Act Three: What Am I? 151

tion? This means you, directing yourself to deliver the speech in a real and expressive way.

What of you is in the material you chose?

What do you need to communicate to yourself from the material you chose?

What are you telling yourself about a next step for you?

## Scene Nine
## *The Energy Involved in Self-Communion*

As sap travels through a mighty tree providing life-force and communicating with every branch and leaf, and back again to the roots, so vital life-force (prana) moves through us from energy center (chakra) to energy center (chakra) enabling us to communicate with self and then with others. During self-communion one center interacts with another. As a result we become aware of an intention and we choose to give it expression.

Two such centers might be the crown chakra (consciousness) and the solar plexus chakra (feelings), or the heart chakra (unconditional love) and the gernerative chakra (creativity and action). If, for example, in your heart center you feel a rush of love and compassion for yourself in a given moment, you could, through the generative chakra, forgive yourself for something or express kindness to yourself in a special way.

Conscious communion within self allows you to hold active intercourse with emerging feelings and to direct them into expression. This same intercourse is what transpires between you and another.

## Act Three: What Am I? 153

When you are aware of the vital life-force moving through you, you can have jurisdiction over how to give it expression.

When the communion is there in self, it projects outward and can be registered and absorbed by others. This exchange becomes explicit when you speak, but the energy flow remains real and strong between the words. Sustained conscious flow is conscious presence to prana.

It is rare to have an unbroken flow from frequency registry (or chakra sensing) to a series of feelings which does not awaken something in you. More often than not, because of your identification with character, you glom onto a given feeling and take it personally. You then get stuck in that feeling and cease to communicate in a flow. You engage with another while remaining in your own box of feelings. You appear to be listening as one character to another but you are merely waiting for your cue to speak, and when you do, you speak not from the registry of what is transpiring between you and the other but from what you are identified with in your own private world that you call "feelings."

If you engage only with your own thoughts and feelings you remain in a private world to which no one else has access. A private world engaging is an event of separation happening in the illusion of togetherness. Being true to frequency allows for a penetrating throughline of communion that happens freshly in the moment.

The flow of energy is from frequency, to experience, to expression, without personalizing by tying into history, as in: "I know how you're going to react to this." The life-artist comes to know that both the character through whom he relates and the character to whom he relates are the medium (an intervening substance through which something is transmitted or carried on) for frequency connection.

Self-communication can only occur when you are focused, aware, and choosing to direct your life force. You know that **you don't just *have* feelings; in fact, you *create* them and you *choose* the degree of energy with which you infuse each feeling.** When you are in the middle of an emotional experience this is not as easy to do. You "get caught up" in the event and forget that you have any creative jurisdiction. To practice remaining focused and aware while directing your life force, it is helpful to begin with simple life examples. Here is one you might like to try.

### *Exercise:*

Lie down on the floor on your back with your hands at your sides, palms down, and your eyes closed. Turn your attention to your breath, breathing in and out slowly, fully, and steadily, relaxing your body and your mind.

After a short while, focus your attention on the very tip of the pinky finger of your right hand. Don't move it but begin to send energy from beyond the top of your head (the crown chakra) down on the throughline to the tip of that finger. See if you can feel heat accumulating there.

## Act Three: What Am I? 155

Then proceed, ever so slowly, to send energy to the tip and then from there to the first knuckle, and then continuing up the finger until the whole of it is being consciously filled with the energy you are directing. Be aware that that finger feels different from the others on your hand.

After a short while, begin sending energy to the remaining fingers on the right hand and then to the palm and then to the wrist. By now you will experience how different the hand feels from the rest of the arm and the rest of your body. It will be more alive, maybe even tingling, maybe hot.

Begin to change the event by breathing in and exhaling through the hand, reversing the process. Start with the wrist and breathe out through the wrist, then through the palm, then through the fingers, all the way down to where you began with the tip of the pinky finger.

You might feel increased sensation or warmth in each of the areas. You will certainly feel greater life than when you are not consciously directing your energy.

This little exercise is designed to allow you to experience the power you have when consciously directing your energy. Magnified you can see how you could use this skill during sports activities, during tasks such as lifting heavy objects, and in a myriad of other physical ways. Carried a step further, you will be able to choose how much energy you put in the creation of a feeling and be the guide of the imprint it makes in an interaction.

Once during a hotel stay, a man entered my room in the middle of the night. He may have been drunk and thought it was his room. By some fluke his key worked in my door. I woke from my sleep instantly and bolted straight up in bed. I screamed as loud as I could and he flew backward as if blown by a hurricane force.

If I had simply screamed in fear the energy would have been diffused and chaotic. Instead, the scream carried directed energy that said loud and clear, GET OUT OF HERE! And he did.

The process used in directing energy to the tip of a finger is the very same that was used in the scream. The life force flew across the room from the bed to the door as if it had been a spear. That is powerful communication.

## Scene Ten
# What Am I? How Do I Communicate with Myself?

You need all of who you are for full communion. You need to learn how to use all you have as an instrument of expression in order for the vital life force to be fully expended. Your vehicle is the means of expression of rays of energy. The rays are tangible much beyond the limits of the form of your body if conscious transmission on the throughline is occurring.

Intensity of ray-energy has a much greater chance of radiating when there is no excess tension. Excess tension "traps" the energy in a familiar expression and restricts discovery.

### Exercise:
Try this out by telling another person about someone you love dearly and why. Hold the loved one in the seat of consciousness and breathe the person into your solar plexus and out in feeling.

Your objective is to direct the energy rays you are registering. Have your partner practice absorbing the rays rather than just hearing the words you are saying. Make sure there is no excess tension in either of you.

See if you experience the underground river of energy which flows continuously under the surface of words and forms an invisible bond between the two of you. Try this not only with a specific partner but in a variety of situations when you are speaking or listening.

In order to transmit, you must experience what you are transmitting. Physical sensations will be present, but barely perceptible compared to the force of the current that flows in you and through you. Be conscious of the greater inner activity of prana (energy) moving.

## *Exercise:*

Here is a major experience for you to try in order to further your discovery of what you are. This will be a journey into the intangible: from Player frequency registry to character expression through the embodiment of feeling and the activation of a primary quality.

*Your purpose is* **to enhance the capacity to feel and express feeling.**

*Your objectives are:*

**To communicate** with self from the center of consciousness (crown chakra) to the center of feeling (the solar plexus)

**To discover** the more that is waiting to open in and through you

### Act Three: What Am I? 159

**To break through** to a next level of knowing

1. Begin the day by preparing your body through stretches, quieting your mind, and opening yourself to the unknown.

2. Sit in silence, breathing and registering frequencies.

3. Focus on your life purpose, and then choose an overall objective with which to work.

   Next, choose either the generative or heart chakra to support you as you seek to feel and express more deeply through the solar plexus chakra.

   Breathe into the frequency of the two chosen chakras and select a quality to manifest through your character which will facilitate feeling and expressing feeling. It may be one you are afraid of, unfamiliar with, feel blocked in relation to, or want to develop. You might choose a quality such as courage, or gentleness, or loving, or powerful, or carefree, or bold, or daring, or emerging. There are endless qualities from which to choose.

4. Enhance the quality through the clothes you choose and the environment you create in which you can move and embody the qual-

ity, your objective, your supportive chakra, and above all, your solar plexus. Pay special attention to colors and textures, and choose music to play. The environment should fit the quality you are activating. Bring into it whatever will serve you to embody that quality.

5. Immerse yourself in the objective, the chakra, the quality (you will now be immersing yourself in a frequency), and your solar plexus. Select or write a poem that communicates the quality, the objective and the chakra, and enables you to merge with them.

6. Choreograph and rehearse ten specific and different movements that allow your body and personality to fully become that quality and to embody the objective and express through the chakra.

7. In the environment, practice talking aloud to yourself about how you experience yourself beginning to be able to embody this quality and what you have to change in yourself in order to do that more fully.

Choose two persons in your life in relation to whom you feel blocked energy (living or dead) and in relation to whom you want to let feelings flow freely. Bring them into your environment in your imagination one at a

## Act Three: What Am I? 161

time and practice relating to them thorough the objective, chakra, quality, and solar plexus by moving in your body in new ways in relation to each of them and by talking aloud to yourself about regrets, guilt, sorrows, anger, hopes, etc. you are holding in relation to them.

As you practice, allow insights and feelings to flow fully. Fully immerse yourself in the expression of feelings. At the height of that expression, ask yourself: What do I need to do to become freer, to express with greater power, to allow my feelings to flow unrestricted? See what comes to you. It may appear as a new quality of being. When you see it, immediately embody it, give it life, give it sound. Feel and experience the difference in yourself.

Expand this by asking yourself: What most holds me back from fulfilling my life purpose? Or, what unfinished business in my life constricts me and holds me bound in patterned responses through character?

8. Speak aloud to yourself about all of this. Speak about what you see to do to move through this to something more, something you don't yet see but can feel just beyond your reach – describe what you sense, its essence, its qualities. Take the physical shape of this "more" and begin to move in

what you sense and make the sound of it.

What is calling to you? What is the more that is just beyond your awareness? Give it shape with your body and movement and sound. Let your body and being take you and show you what is emerging. Stay out of your head and go with the new. Surprise yourself. Then see if you can describe the new that has emerged, the qualities that accompany it, and what changes you will have to activate in your life to move through what holds you back, into the more that is emerging.

9. Allow yourself to break through to greater freedom and new ways of functioning.

Remember the textures, colors, and qualities that allowed you to move to new levels. Use them in the coming days to enhance the greater expression of self you are ready to embody.


Remember, when you are semi-conscious, you are in your own way. When you are conscious, you not only are not in your way, you are the way.

## Scene Eleven
## *Oneness*

An organic bond exists between body and Player, between character and Player. Similarly, there can be an organic bond between each of us. We need to feel our way into the rays being emitted and we will become One because we will be present simultaneously to the same frequency. This is what Oneness is. It is not Oneness with another person, though that is how we often primarily identify our experience.

Oneness is simultaneity of frequency registry, and not the glamour of "I," as in I, character, am One with your character. Yet, it is through character that the expressions of connection are made. The process itself is intuitive and natural.

We live in a dynamic field of Life Force, Prana. It is moving through each of us and between all of us. We are all energy beings. What Am I? I am energy, inseparable from the energy field around me. I am one with all that is.

# ACT FOUR

## Why Am I?

"I have the power to move through resistance and stop it from getting in the way of my personal growth. Before **Theatre of Life,** I thought there were things I couldn't do because they weren't 'me.' Now I know that I can do or be whatever I choose."
— *Robyn Runbeck, Paradise Valley, AZ*

"This has been the most transformative experience of the past ten years of my life. The theme for me was to say yes to myself, to hone the divine urges, and to infuse them with enough feeling to give life to them. I connected with the spiritual throughline at a new level and am now much more able to stay connected. The entire process has given me much more creative jurisdiction over my entire life and functioning. Never again will I let myself settle into comfortable unconsciousness."
— *Scott Miller, Albuquerque, NM*

"I was pleased with how often I was able to catch my attention being drawn outside myself and bring it back inside again. I believe it was the first time that I was able to sustain that level of awareness. I have learned that reality is entirely subjective because it is filtered through each individual's past history. What we believe to be true is the reality for us and if we don't create it consciously we create it unconsciously."
— *Maggie Hissam, Chagrin Falls, OH*

"One major learning about my character was the pervasiveness and destructiveness of her accommodator pattern. I practiced standing up for myself, stating my opinions and feelings, and even arguing. My fear of fully expressing myself often stemmed from a fear of rejection, though when I remain silent, I am essentially rejecting myself. I think rejection of self is more deadly to me."
— *Dianne Grassé, Chandler, AZ*

"Knowing I am Player creating and expressing through character opens endless possibilities for change and fine frequency work. It is so very simple and clear. I am free to choose."
— *Leila Whitcombe, Mt. Shasta, CA*

## Scene One
# Why Am I Here?

During this Act, four basic questions will be explored.

- Why am I here in relation to the whole? What does my uniqueness contribute?
- Why have I created this particular character structure through which to experience my world and make manifest what I register in frequency?
- What are the underlying threads that weave my character patterns together? How do they serve me; how do I use or abuse them?
- What is my life purpose and how does it relate to my internal learning agenda for this lifetime?

These questions demand serious reflection. It is not often we ask, "Why am I here?" Most of the time we coast through our lives. We are here but we have no idea why or even that there is a reason. We get out of bed and sleep walk through our activities and relationships. We do this day after day, unless we are confronted by a challenge which jolts us into examination or reflection.

Each of us is a minute part of the whole and we each have our unique contribution to make so that the whole remains functional and growing. We must begin to think of ourselves as unique, identify what makes us different, and consciously make the contribution that is ours to make.

We each function through a character or personality that is different from all other people. When we are conscious we know that we have created the character. In fact, we are still creating and recreating it to match who we know ourselves to be and how we wish to be seen and known. All of this must be done with awareness and choice-making because if the outer doesn't reflect the inner, we are not coherent representations of ourselves.

Every character pattern emerges from underlying influences in our lives. How we are treated by others often leads to the degree of openness or self-protection we develop, for example. Knowing how the threads come into being and are activated enables us to decide whether to keep them in the fabric of self or to choose new ones that serve us more effectively.

Most of us are familiar with setting goals for ourselves. They represent what we want to "get" or accomplish. Yet, goals are fleeting when compared with having a purpose and knowing how that purpose relates to what your soul seeks to achieve in this lifetime. Having a purpose and objectives for the day keeps us focused and enables us to direct our life force. Knowing your life purpose gives you a

### Act Four: Why Am I?

large grid on which to lay out your purposes for this time period and for each day. Having a life purpose is akin to viewing your existence from the perspective of outer space. You can see your place in the whole and you can determine the imprint you need to be making as you live and breathe.

## Scene Two
## *Adapting*

One way of discovering *Why Am I* is through seeing how willing or unwilling you are to adapt to life in a given moment, and how capable or incapable of adaptation you are.

Adaptation is the inner and outer means that people use to adjust themselves to one another in a variety of relationships. It also helps to bring objectives into being. Throughout the day you adapt to circumstances, the times, individual persons, and events. This is true even if you live alone. When the temperature changes, your body has to change. You always have to adapt.

In **Theatre of Life** terms, to adapt means to meet.

You bring forth different facets of yourself to meet the different life circumstances that present themselves to you. To meet should immediately call to mind the equality of peers.

This next phrase is absolutely key to all your work in Act Four: to adapt self is a creative way of reaching from the wholeness of self to union with another (meaning others or other than self). Implied then is, to meet.

## Act Four: Why Am I? 171

Whenever you put yourself into a wholly natural, relaxed state, there wells up within you a flow of creative force that is almost blinding in its brilliance. This is when you do nothing about bringing something into being and it's all there. You release resistance, suppose-to's, and the hard work of making something happen. What's left after all of that is that you become one with what is. You become what you are looking for with no effort.

How do you do this? How do you refrain from interfering with Nature and avoid contravention of her laws? How do you know what the natural order is, especially without conjuring it up in your mind? If it is invented by the mind then you connect with your own image of the natural order and settle for aligning with it: image over reality.

You adapt to the natural order by reaching from your inner wholeness. To do this kind of reaching your objective must be to find the most direct way of crossing the gap between you and other. Find the most direct way to move on the throughline. The clearer the objective in a given moment, the more direct the way.

To adapt is to find the most direct way of reaching another. In adaptation, then, we move forward from the core of self to meet what is coming from the other. Note that any receiving begins with what and how you are sending. You reach, you register, and you meet.

Observe yourself as you move through the day. When do you adapt? How do you adapt? Do you experience the meeting with others?

## Scene Three
## *The Life Story*

The focus of your primary work in Act Four will be on an in-depth look into your own life story and what it appears to be about. Throughout your work on the life story, the key principle to hold in mind is "have no expectations." This will lead to constant discovery. Do not try to anticipate anything.

Function in abundant expectancy. This is to live as a breathing dynamic pulsation in the midst of the void. The void is not the hum of death that goes across the heart monitor when the patient is gone. It is the rumble that is the essence of the Life Force in its dance in the Universe. We participate in the emerging unknown by bringing the whole of our consciousness to the pulsing, to the presence of possibility.

Resist any speculation. Speculation results in dissipation. Speculation is foreplay with no intention of climax.

Work on your life story will test your ability to stay in the now moment and refrain from anticipating. Your discipline is to do only what is asked of you and not jump ahead.

Every bit of input that I give you in this Act will be applied to the character in your life story.

## Act Four: Why Am I? 173

As we begin, keep your work on your life story in a separate notebook so that you can follow what you learn about yourself.

***Exercise:***
Your first task is to make a one-sentence statement of the story of your life. For example, "This is a story about overcoming fear and shyness," or "This is a story about waking up to discover my real self," or "This is a story about emerging into full expression." To help you with the on-going process of discovery, I will use myself as an example. It will be an invitation to you to peer into your own life and find your own answers.

As you proceed, write in the third-person, using "she or he" rather than I, so that the story you are developing is about a character one step removed from you. She or he is a mirror into which you can look to see how a life is developed. As the life unfolds, don't draw analytical comparisons such as, "Oh, I see how this is connected to this." Instead, discover connections beyond the level of understanding. The level on which to connect is feeling/knowing.

Take a deep breath. Move into abundant expectancy with every cell alive, alert. Write your one-sentence statement of the story of your life.

Now read the sentence aloud to yourself.

Take a moment to see if you had any feelings,

thoughts, or sensations while reading this sentence and make a note of them.

*In my case, for example*, This is a life story about a creative person in search of her true expression.

I feel a sense of excitement. I am pleased that she is a creative person. I wonder what avenues she will choose. I wonder what her specific talents are. I can hear the big pot on the stove, bubbling with possibilities.

Write down your feelings, thoughts and sensations.

## Scene Four
# *Motivating Forces*

You are living your life through a body and through character. Both are your own creations and both can be altered depending on your degree of consciousness. You are not the body. You are not the character. You are Player who has, or can have, creative jurisdiction over both.

The character (which includes the character's body) is the instrument on which the virtuoso Player performs. The instrument needs to be finely tuned and ready to be played. You play it with your imagination, your attention, and with your feelings. Stanislavski said: "Feel the life part you are playing and instantly all your inner chords will harmonize. Your whole bodily apparatus of expression will begin to function."

To do this, allow yourself to suffer no interference. Put up no resistance. Enter the void of creation. It's as if you were a pocket and you no longer chose to be hidden in the trousers. You turn yourself inside out and expose the whole of yourself to life. The character needs to be ready to be played. It is here to serve Player.

We are embodied in order to:

1. register frequencies,
2. exercise consciousness, and
3. activate the will.

**Registry of Frequency** and alignment with frequency leads to the harmonious sounding of all the inner chords. This allows the body to function as an instrument of expression. The character identifies frequencies through experience and as experience: feelings, thoughts, actions, sensations. Consciousness = the activity of frequency.

We catch a reflection of the direct experience of frequency registry. For example: we feel an urge. We open to that urge and give it expression, sometimes through movement, sometimes through poetry, or in a myriad of ways. We are more conscious of the expression of the urge (the reflection of the experience of frequency registry) than we are of the urge itself.

Urges call to us, lead us, often awaken us. My own cosmic breakthrough occurred in just this way. First, I had a sense that something was calling to me, but I had no idea what it was. (It was good that I had no "idea" because what was calling was not on the mental level. Any picture I would have conjured up on that mental level would not have matched what was calling, which was as yet unknown to me.)

Then, I was drawn to a flower. I bent to admire it and suddenly I felt myself shift from the physical view of the flower into an energy frequency experience of the flower. The flower itself disappeared as

## Act Four: Why Am I? 177

I shifted from an outer to an inner view. I experienced myself as energy and began to enter and merge with the energy of the flower. We became one. I immediately knew that everything in the universe is of one being, everything is energy.

When **we function consciously**, Player registers the stirring, the movement in the energy world. Consciousness is the activity of the frequency. We catch a reflection of the direct experience of frequency registry. To catch means we hold it in something we call time. We give ourselves the time to become aware of what we are registering. What we are registering is a reflection of the direct experience. Consciousness awakens awareness. Awareness is like a reflector. It throws its rays on a chosen subject. This arouses our thoughts, feelings, desires, memories. The character identifies frequencies as consciousness.

Once frequency registry and consciousness are in place, we move to **activate the Will**. The Will directs creative action. The Will infuses frequencies that were consciously registered with the impetus to manifest. The character identifies the Will as determination.

We see too much calculated life, scenic life productions of intellectual origin. We rarely see true, living creativity. When the three forces (frequency registry, consciousness, and the Will) cooperate harmoniously we can create freely.

Experiences that come through the activation

of these three forces are indelibly imprinted on us. They are life-changing. They motivate us to take our next steps in our spiritual unfolding.

## *Exercise:*

Return now to your life story. Make a list of life-changing events after which nothing was ever again the same in your life. Group them into Acts and Scenes: Act One, Act Two, Act Three. Doing this will help you to see more clearly why you are here and to discover what motivates you to continue.

*In my own example,* I would call Act One the period of childhood through adolescence. Act Two would represent the time period before Awakening. Act Three would be the period when I consciously directed my life.

In Act One, Scene One the life-changing events would include the day my mother took so much time tossing a coin to me from our apartment window that I missed the merry-go-round ride. On that day I vowed I would never again be controlled by anyone.

From there I would go on listing other life-changing events during the childhood period. These would provide me with a startling picture of how I shaped my world based on my responses to events and circumstance.

In Act Two, a life-changing event occurred at age 29 when I suffered heart disease and my life hung in the balance.

Act Three scenes would include my awakening flower experience, the time I saw myself from a vantage point atop the Canadian Rockies as I rode in a car far below, and another scene in which I was taken to spiritual classes during my sleep where I relearned the wisdom I had known and was able to bring that wisdom into consciousness.

Do your own breakdown of three Acts and the Scenes within the Acts, so that you can see how your life story has unfolded.

For each Act, identify the key event that marks the curtain falling on that Act. That key event or moment will hold "the audience's interest" and keep them coming back for more. That key event will also hold your interest and keep you coming back to discover the motivating factors in your life story.

*For example,* in my own life: Act One would end with me having a triumphant success while directing a play in summer camp. I was at the height of my creativity at age 19 and felt the whole world would open up to me and I would soon star on Broadway.

Act Two would end with me weighing 96 pounds, having practically no life force, and not knowing if I would live to be 30.

Act Three would end... you get the point.

See what you come up with and write it all down.

## *Exercises:*

In addition, here are some other exercises to help you practice registering frequencies consciously.

1. Put on some music and stand listening to it with your eyes closed. Direct your attention outward to the music, adapting to it, reaching toward it, coming to meet it. Merge with the music, become one with it. Let it move you. Let it take you as you come to meet it. Let yourself be moved by what your inner eye sees. With the seeing comes the movement at one and the same moment.

2. Repeat the listening, but this time be in stillness within and in your body as well. Listen with all your cells, without moving. Then, allow yourself to move again.

3. Smell your way into a plant or flower and merge with it. Also, eat something sumptuous. Fill your mouth with it. Chew every taste, merging with the taste until you become what you are chewing.

4. Stand in the shower with your eyes closed and move into the frequency of the rushing water until you give the whole of yourself to the rush of the water and merge with it.

## Scene Five
## *Objectives*

Looking at your life as a story puts a frame around it. As with a stage play, the story is more confined than life, which tends to sprawl. The life story must begin and end in the given time frame and something must happen, some change must occur in that speeded up time.

In life, we indulge ourselves in endless moments of non-change. You are the author of your life story. Hence, you are the like the playwright who develops the character. In this case, you, as Player, are the one who develops the character.

### *Exercise:*
Take a look at what you have written thus far, reading it (aloud, if you like), telling the story and the key events. This is the main plot, revealed by you because you, better than anyone, know what this life is about.

What is your life about? What is your life purpose? What objectives are you giving life in order to fill that life purpose?

These three questions are among the most important you will answer if you want to live a directed, meaningful life. Without focusing on purpose and objective, one day simply blends into the next and you fall into relationships or a career without satisfying the deep longing of your soul because you don't know what it is.

What is your life purpose? You will find clues to this in what your life story seems to be about and in the key happenings in each of the three Acts.

*In my own case,* my life purpose is to serve the creative process. That purpose is like a large umbrella. Serving the creative process can be done in many ways and it is for me to discover which of those ways is most fulfilling. I can choose a career to be the main thrust of my contribution to creativity, but I also need small ways, objectives, to keep the creative flow going in my everyday life.

Objectives are the active expression of purpose. They move us from moment to moment. Purpose is larger than objectives. Purpose moves us through an entire life-cycle.

Purpose and objectives can be seen as rays of energy. These rays of energy are cast from Player into and through the character. Player registers the purpose, chooses the objectives from the purpose, and then expresses them through character manifestation.

If you are having trouble identifying your life purpose, have a look back at the events in the three Acts and work your way backwards.

What was Player's overall objective (what did

## Act Four: Why Am I? 183

you want to have happen) in each Act? Once you identify this, you will begin to see a picture unfolding of your life purpose and how each objective contributed to the fulfilling of that.

Do your best to come up with a working statement of your life purpose. Make the statement very large, something that can keep you interested for decades and never really be fully achieved.

Beyond determining a life purpose, there is a Super-Objective. This cannot really be consciously known to us but we can catch glimpses of it. While Player enables character to find a life purpose and objectives for fulfilling it, Super-Objective comes from a high realm, we might say from the One to Player. This Super-Objective is the main focus for the plot of the life being lived.

The Super-Objective is what is wanted of us, as differentiated from what we want. It is similar for each of us yet different. It's different because it's heard differently through each Player. None of us has knowledge of the whole. We are a part of the whole.

The Super-Objective is an inner line that guides us from the beginning to the end of the life play. In the life story you are working on, the Super-Objective is your throughline. It pulls together all the small units and objectives of the life story. This can be called The Journey Home. In life you utilize consciousness to define purpose, design objectives, and move in a forward direction. This is the journey home. You are on your way to the Super-Objective.

You need a throughline of action so as to avoid

being governed by disjointed steps which serve only for a moment. It would be like having the bits and pieces of a beautiful sculpture but never seeing the whole work.

All minor lines are headed toward the same goal. They fuse into one main current.

Conflict takes us forward. Life thrives on problems/opportunities. What happens in life is that every action meets with a re-action which in turn intensifies the first. What you resist, persists. And this relates to adaptation. You have a constant intensification period going on with every life moment. You adapt by meeting it and going forward to reach it, not by retreating from it. You bring it your unique response which furthers the action of the life story. And in every life story there is always counter action to the main action. Without counter action nothing would happen. These conflicts cause activity which is the basis of creativity.

## *Exercise:*

Write a working statement of your life purpose. Then, look at each Act and give it an overall objective.

The key events in each Act represent the given circumstances of your life at that time (what actually happened.) Ask yourself and record,

>1. What happened to, for, and in my character in this Act?
>
>2. What was my objective?

3. What did I want?

Now, identify the other key characters in each Act, without whom the plot could not have unfolded in the way it did.

To get a different perspective on the event you have chosen in each act, step inside the reality of one other key person in the event and, from that person's point of view, to the best of your ability, ask and answer the same questions: What happened to me, for me, in me (as this other person)? What was my objective? What did I want?

Doing this might well give you an entirely new way to see what was going on in this event.

## Scene Six
## *Being Guided by the Unknown Super-Objective*

If you allow yourself to hold in the back of your consciousness the question, "What is wanted of me?" you will find little clues in everything you do. If you are aware of your defined life purpose every day, your life will move along on fundamental lines of direction.

### *Exercise:*
With your life purpose in mind, close your eyes, breathe and center yourself. Choose one Act, and breathe into an awareness of yourself now, as well as the character you were playing in the life story then, so that both are here and present for you. Continuing to breathe, allow yourself to be present to the swirl of all you know about this character then, and all you know about the life story up to that point. Be present without calling up details. Based on all you know of this character you were then and the one you are now, allow to come into your consciousness what may be a possible Super-

## Act Four: Why Am I?

Objective for this play character's life and write it down.

Write this down on a fresh page. This is your working page for the Super-Objective. It is your first step of reaching toward it.

### *Exercise:*
To learn more about the character then and the character now, write a dialogue. Begin with a question to the character of then, or a statement from you now, and respond to each other. Let the dialogue run as long as is productive.

## Scene Seven
# The Unbroken Line

There are three key features in the creative process.

First is an **Inner Grasp** — of the given circumstance, of what is happening to the character, and of the objectives being played out by the character. Inner grasp can be translated as registry of frequency.

Second is a **Throughline of Action** — doing what is called for by the purpose and the objectives, through activities. Rather than getting stuck in what is happening in the character, focus on what is happening *through* the character.

Third is the **Activation of the Will** — giving self the wherewithal to bring the task to fruition.

Until Player's purpose is clear, the direction of the character actions will remain erratic. Moments of consciousness and alignment will be few and far between. Thoughts, feelings, and desires will appear and disappear like indistinct persons in a large, fast moving crowd. The pattern of the life course will be disjointed and broken. It is only when you come to a deeper understanding of the part you are playing in this life moment and a realization of its fundamental objective that a line gradually emerges as a continuous whole. You are then living as an artist in a creative process.

The throughline is broken and disjointed when thoughts, feelings, and desires appear and disappear in a disjointed way. As purpose emerges, so does a continuous flow of consciousness. When this unbroken line is present, true creative action begins.

There will always be interruptions to the line. Yet during those breaks, a person continues to exist. Therefore some sort of line continues. Indeed, you have many lines to represent the direction of your various inner activities. Having an unbroken line gives life and movement to what is being enacted. Let the line be interrupted and life stops being lived creatively. Let it be revived and life goes on with a vibrant flow.

This spasmodic dying away and reviving is a reflection of slipping in and out of consciousness. To live as an artist you must have continuous presence in an unbroken line. The life of a person consists of continuous choices of objectives and of circles of attention, on the plane of reality or of the imagination, and in the realm of memories of the past or in dreams about the future.

The strength of this solid line is of utmost importance to you as a life-artist. It is an unending chain of different points. Your attention is constantly passing from one point of view to another. You sustain your line of attention by consciously moving from one focus to the next. If you fixed your attention on one idea, thought, or feeling during a whole life scene you would be spiritually unbalanced because there would be no organic flow of energy.

From the primary line of Player purpose, there extends a web of lines called objectives — for life periods, for days, for moments. If you live in the web without larger purpose, your life becomes a series of meaningless activities for their own sake.

## *Exercise:*

As you look at your life story, see if you can find an even clearer statement of your life purpose and identify the objectives that have served to move your life forward. You should be able to identify an objective for each of the major events in each scene, for example.

## Scene Eight
## *How Our Lives Are Affected by Others*

You can learn about yourself by observing how you function in relation to others. For you to have a healthy exchange there needs to be balance, give and take, and mutual nourishment. If you play the role of people-pleaser, you may think you are creating excellent relationships but this will not be so. If you are not true to yourself, if you yield on what is important to you in order to keep the peace, you may give yourself away.

There is a big difference between **adapting** and **accommodating.**

To adapt is to be true to yourself while giving to another. When you adapt, you reach to the other and seek to meet halfway in the exchange. To reach is to be responsive to self first and then to the other. You are responsive to the frequencies you are registering and you reach forth from those, being true to the natural order process that you are experiencing within your own consciousness.

Why Am I? I Am in order to be responsive to

what I am registering and to give it unique life as only I can.

To accommodate is to abandon self in order to please the other and to keep from making waves. When you accommodate you are responding to what the other wants or needs, and leaving yourself out of the picture. While this may feel virtuous, since you are thinking of the other rather than of yourself, you are not really giving of yourself to the other. You have left yourself behind and have made yourself into what the other desires. You might as well not be there.

## *Exercise:*

Look at your three Acts and identify a key character in each one without whom the plot could not have unfolded in the way it did.

Describe how you were affected by this key character, how you were imprinted and how this influenced choices you made.

Now assess whether you adapted or accommodated.

If you accommodated in any way, abandoning your own center to make concessions, write about how that occurred so that you might reinforce your learning in this regard. Then, do a fantasy reflection to see how the events of this Act might have been different if you had adapted instead.

## Scene Nine
## *Discovering the Character's Makeup*

When you attend a play, you get to observe the character development of each person on the stage. As you observe how they interact with each other you gather information about why they exist and what they contribute to the whole. Without them there would not be a play. With them, the play moves in a particular direction because of who they are and how they interact with each other.

When you attend to a life, namely yours, the same dynamic occurs. It is important, therefore, to be aware of your own character development, how you interact with others, how you make choices, and what life-play is unfolding, because you are writing it as you go.

Character study is a study of the character's essence. The essence of your own character is a reflection of what you, as Player, have brought into being to fulfill your part in the whole.

In order to more clearly formulate the answer to the question "Why Am I?" it is key that you know what elements you have incorporated into your character expression. Your role in the whole is reflected in the pieces or threads of the whole that you have selected out to embody. You may not have done this consciously in the past but you can perhaps do some of this now, in reflection.

## *Exercise:*

At this point, I encourage you to use some of the techniques from Acts One, Two, and Three to explore the threads you chose. For example, select an animal, from memory, that fits the essence of how you lived during Act One of your life story. Give it life in movement and sound so that you can have a live experience of what influenced your choices. Or, with Act Two of your life story, use your Act Two experience by going to the library art section and choosing a painting that embodies the primary colors and styles of behavior that were prevalent in your life story then. Or, in Act Three of your life story, see what feelings predominated. Give them life in your body and in sound and then reflect on how those feelings motivated you.

Make notes in your journal of the basic elements (qualities and characteristics) that make up the essence of your character.

## Scene Ten
## *The Inner Creative State*

As Player, you bring your character's outer life into being just the way a painter brings life to a canvas. Instead of paints and brushes, Player uses frequency registry and brings life expression into being through feeling. Feeling combines with consciousness and will to mobilize the inner creative forces which enable you to carry out your life purpose.

The character is the facet of self that experiences limitations. It thinks it can't take it anymore, it can't give anymore, it can't go any further. And every time it says that, it is asking for further instructions from Player, which sees the More, knows the More, and knows no limitations, ever, because it functions in frequency.

In life, all too often you have a running script in your private world. You wait for another character in the life dynamic to finish speaking so that you can have a chance to say your lines, which you have already rehearsed while they were speaking and you seemed to be listening. You often don't register what the other is saying, because you are so busy getting ready to say your own lines.

There is a big difference between getting tangled in your private world and being fully present in a silent self, registering what is transpiring, feeling an urge to respond, and then offering your unique gift of self. Functioning this way, the interaction between the two of you can be lifted to a level you could not have conceived in your thoughts.

Until now you may not have been aware that you had a script running in your private world. There is a way to bring this into the light of consciousness.

## *Exercise:*

Engage with a friend about what is transpiring in both your lives. Invite your friend to join you in a process of "talking thoughts."

"Talking thoughts" is fleshing out the undercurrent of dialog. It is to speak out here in the open, everything that is going on in your private world. What normally happens is that you speak something on the surface while another track is running underneath and you are censoring what comes out. Here you are to speak everything out loud. It is a way of telling yourself, as well as the other, what you are saying, what you are really saying between the lines.

You will both say everything you are thinking and feeling about what you are saying. Intersperse the thoughts and feelings with the words you are saying. The conversation the two of you will have will be far richer and it will lead you to a depth of relationship you didn't have before. This is a process of revealing your inner process to yourself and allowing it to be seen by others.

## Act Four: Why Am I? 197

A life of truth is lived when the outer expressions are a direct reflection of the inner purpose. If your character choices are artificial, truth becomes adherence to conventional patterns, as in "This is who I am and you have to accept me this way." Rather than registering and manifesting, you imitate or allow old patterns to live in your life space. Functioning in a true inner creative state precludes falling into habits of artificiality.

You are the pitcher from which the vital life force pours through the cells of the manifested representation.

The inner creative state is fueled by choosing active objectives to move energy and life forward. It is through objectives, which align with your life purpose, that you can give direction to your character. Even though you don't really know what the Super-Objective is for your life, what is wanted makes itself known through your life purpose.

It always helps to remind yourself of who you are, what you want to do (objective), and how you can do it (activity or action).

The life actor weeps and laughs on life's stage and all the while is watching the tears and the smiles. It is this double function, this balance between what seems to be life and the conscious enacting of life that makes for artful living.

Don't take your character and life so seriously that you become totally absorbed by it, identified with it.

What "happens" to us daily through character interactions with the world are the given circumstances of the life play. Each circumstance needs to be brought under the view of our purpose. It is the stimulant for the organizing of your inner forces. This is done most effectively through choosing facilitative objectives.

If your objectives are clean-cut and your action is directed, your inner state will be solid. If your objectives are vague, your inner state is likely to be fragile.

Preparation is key to the inner creative process, especially preparing the instrument — the inner self and the body. To prepare, you activate your will, focus on your objective, and direct your energy to the task.

## *Act Four Extended Practice*

Here is an optional experience you might like to try, especially if you have access to plays and you have a partner who would like to do serious work with you.

## *Steps for Working on a Scene*

### *Step One:*

Choose a play with characters that will stretch each of you and give each of you a chance to work on character development directly while simultaneously working impersonally.

Read the play for content only.

Read the play a second time to determine what the author is trying to make as a point and how each character is used and each circumstance is used to achieve this.

Then read the play once more. This time focus on the character you will be playing and what its primary and secondary characteristics are. What does this character think of self? What does every other character say or think about this character? What does this character do to further the author's premise/theme? What does this character need/want and how does she/he go about specifically getting it? And lastly, what is the character's overall purpose?

## Step Two:
Tell the story of the plot of the play to each other.

## Step Three:
Choose one scene to play out together. Dialog with your character. Ask it questions, let it speak to you. Do explorations dealing with past and future (the present always occurs on stage). Answer questions such as Where did I come from? Where am I going? What happened between the times I was on stage?

Invent future and past experiences and tell them to each other as stories. Have your partner tell you what feelings and sensations were evoked in him or her.

### Step Four:
Discuss the given circumstances of the scene as each of you sees it. What is happening here? What is happening to me, for me, in me, through me? What is my overall objective in the scene?

### Step Five:
Based on all you know of the character, draft a Super-Objective for her/his life.

### Step Six:
Work with your partner to break the scene down into the units of change.

### Step Seven:
Do a first reading of the scene together aloud, a reading of discovery.

### Step Eight:
Do a second reading together, writing down actions for each of the units.

All the while you are working on your own character development: using music, clothing, a painting, an animal. It is for you to discover who the character is, not to create it.

### Step Nine:
Beginning here, work in the clothing of the character. Start incorporating your individual character work.

### Step Ten:
Do a third reading aloud on your feet, trying out the actions and changing/adapting them based on what you receive from your partner. Discover activities and physical life that feels appropriate.

### Step Eleven:
Interject talking thoughts and feelings into the text and begin to firm up physical life by experiencing a pattern taking shape.

### Step Twelve:
Do an improvisation on the scene using your own words but playing the basic actions, activities, and physical life.

### Step Thirteen:
Sit perfectly still. Use the author's words to convey the actions, activities, objectives and physical life.

Repeat, free in your chair to use animation, gestures and facial expressions.

Repeat up on your feet, fully embodying the character.

Create a set for the scene.

### Step Fourteen:
Invite in friends and give a performance. Sustain a throughline of inner and outer action and merging with the I AM of this character as you play out the chosen scene.

## Reflections:

What did you learn about yourself as Player during this exercise in which you created a different character from your own?

What similarities and differences did you observe between the play character and your own default character?

What was easiest for you in this experience?

What was most difficult for you in this experience?

Did you make any new discoveries about your life purpose and objectives?

# ACT FIVE

# On What Instrument Do I Play Life's Music?

"Learning the difference between adapting and accommodating will be most helpful to me because I see how the dynamic changes when one is adapting. There is communication on a totally different level. This will be very helpful in all my relationships. Since beginning **Theatre of Life** I have stopped being a door mat."

— *Martha Weatherell, San Benito, TX*

"Act Five increased my appreciation of the connection between power in my voice, breath, body, and feelings. I learned I could speak up and out to another with my own truth, and in love, thus facilitating the other and myself and creating freedom for us both."

— *Helen Cram, Toronto, ON*

"I learned that when each day is lived according to purpose and with objectives, the whole body resonates and is in tune and in harmony. I don't have to step out of my own center to pay attention to the outer world."

— *Karyl Pope, Dundas, ON*

"I learned I can 'bring alive' more characteristics than I thought possible. I see that any pattern, no matter how apparently desirable, is simple to get stuck in if I am not doing it consciously."

— *Patricia Nerison, Port Townsend, WA*

"I have identified characteristics that have been imprisoning me and worked to disarm them. This has given me more self-confidence. I was so shy I had no clue who I was, what my life was about, or how to function in the world and in relation to others. But now I feel fully alive, and I know how to create wholeness within myself. I feel empowered. I have never before been so happy and so full of joy to be alive."

— *Cathleen Young, Williamsville, NY*

"I have been very attached to the faces I have created and have not seen the possibility of creating new ones. I think the key is allowing myself to express feelings, because the tension in my body keeps me feeling suppressed. A transition from character to Player has begun."

— *Sandra Coyne, Aurora, OH*

## Scene One
## *Knowing More About Your Instrument*

In Act Five you begin to discover the unique ways you speak, move, and sound. You will learn how important it is to know your tempo and rhythm, what is in harmony for you, and what isn't.

During this Act you will observe your characteristic ways of functioning during your day-to-day activities. These could be patterns of physical movement, patterns of feeling-responses, patterns of thought processes, or patterns that are a gestalt of all three aspects of character functioning. Do not evaluate the patterns, saying, "This is good and this is bad." Just bring them into consciousness as we move along.

The physical instrument on which you play life's music, namely the body, will constitute much of our focus. If you have been lax about keeping your body in good shape, you may want to begin now doing yoga stretches or other exercises that will promote flexibility and agility and, most especially, that will allow you to begin to know your body as an instrument that serves you in the expression of your life.

And as always, as you begin this Act you will

want to define for yourself your purposes and objectives. You might want to choose as an overall purpose: to break away from attachment to my character as I know it.

## *Exercise:*

I encourage you to begin to listen to the sound of your voice. Is it full, resonant, and strong or is it weak, hoarse, and hidden in the back of your throat? Does your voice carry a frequency that tells others someone of importance is speaking?

Is your speech clear and distinct or do you mumble? Is your choice of words descriptive — even poetic — and filled with meaning, or do you speak in half sentences using one-syllable words that evoke no imagination? Do you communicate and enrich a conversation or is what you say just a filler that is unimpressive?

Watch your body movements. Do your physical expressions convey what you wish to communicate? Are they in alignment with what you are feeling? Do you waste energy in excessive motion?

Is your tempo-rhythm a match for your inner energy flow so that you live your life on a throughline and are not thrown off course by outer events?

Are your primary characteristics of behavior representative of who you are as a being, or do you present a lesser, stylized version of yourself when you are out in the world?

## Act Five: On What Instrument?

You might want to take the time to examine these questions before diving into the work of Act Five so that you come to it with a clearer perspective.

## Scene Two
## *Patterns and Values*

Patterns are convenient when you function unconsciously. They make you feel secure and provide the illusion of centeredness. While there is nothing wrong with this, if you use *only* patterns you function without consciously directing self.

When you guide and direct your energy expenditure, there is power. In contrast, patterns are empty while seeming full. Even worse, you might begin to think of yourself *as* the patterns and then defend your use of them.

Let's say you have a pattern of laughing when you are at a loss for words. The laughter is a cover-up. You defend your use of it because it gets you off the hook. But there is no power in it because no one knows how you really feel. Even you might not know. You defend patterns by saying, "I'm the kind of person who...". This locks you into a way being. You go on being this kind of person without ever re-evaluating.

Patterns come into being because of values you hold and qualities you exhibit to activate your values. You might hold a value of never getting involved in an argument. The pattern that might accompany this is that you shrink from conflict and

## Act Five: On What Instrument?

then support it with a quality of giving in to another's wishes. If you do this, you need to know that this pattern governs you. If you don't know, you can't ever change it.

An important life task is to know who you are and to convey your inner spirit to others through your body and its various communicative means.

### *Exercise:*

Choose a value by which you live and a quality you use to enliven it. Some examples of values are: honesty, commitment, being of service, expressing love, treasuring education. Some examples of qualities are: speaking up for self, caring, being willing, gentleness, concentration.

After choosing a value and a supporting quality, see if you can give these representative life through movement with your body. In this way you get a kinesthetic feel for the value and quality in your life.

Next, add sound to the movement. Is it deep and low or high-pitched? Is it full or very quiet?

Next, call someone on the phone and fully embody the value and the quality, and the sound of both in your words, as you communicate. Note how much richer both are as a result of consciously focusing on them and embodying them.

### *Exercise:*

In order to get a clearer picture of yourself, do

the following exploration of your emotional, physical, mental, and vocal characteristics and your general personality.

What predominant patterns are you aware of in each category in your daily life. Don't judge the patterns, just become familiar with them. See if you can determine the value from which each pattern stemmed. Then see what predominant quality goes with each one.

Before going further in this Act, please rent the film *The Three Faces of Eve.* The film was made in 1957 about a woman who suffered from multiple personality disorder and stars Joanne Woodward, David Wayne, and Lee J. Cobb.

The film will be very helpful to you as you work on the major project of Act Five. You are going to create three faces of your character. You will give them names which can be variations of your own name or descriptive of a pattern that is predominant in your life (e.g. the helpful one or Mr. Busy). These three faces will emerge from facets of your own character self. You have known these facets before but they have been incorporated in bits and pieces in your basic character and exhibited when expedient but have never been developed into a complete individual expression.

You will choose three different contexts (e.g. home, work, a relationship) and assign one to each of the three faces of character. The three contexts are familiar and true to your basic character. They are contexts in which you have exhibited some of

## Act Five: On What Instrument?

these facets, qualities, or characteristics but not as a complete character with a name of its own.

Each character will have its own objective and a bundle of qualities that make it who it is.

As we proceed with Act Five you will write a soliloquy for each character befitting the context you have selected for it. Each should have a very different life from the other.

Toward the end of Act Five I will suggest that you invite in several friends. You will perform the soliloquy for them and you will invite one of those present to participate with you in an improvisation of your design. In the improvisation one of your faces will embody all the appropriate characteristics and interact live with this other person. You will repeat this two more times with two other friends, once for each of the other two faces.

I will provide you with more detailed instructions as we get closer to the performing of this project, but perhaps you can catch a glimpse of the great learning that awaits you when you actually become this face of character, full-blown, and improvise with someone who represents the elements of conflict this face experiences.

For now, watch *The Three Faces of Eve* and see how fully a set of characteristics can take over and become a whole personality.

## Scene Three
## *Characters and Types*

A life actor's instrument is the manifested self, unlike painters who use brushes on a canvas and musicians who use outer instruments to make sound. You play an objective on the manifested self and create subtleties through characteristics. The one thing you don't want to do is limit your range of expression by settling for a few familiar characteristics, patterns, or qualities.

***Exercise:***
Here is an experience for you to try. Choose three different patterns of yours that you want to examine. For each pattern choose three different objectives and a set of qualities you can embody.

*For example,* the pattern might be aggressive behavior. Your objective might be *To Take Over.* Choose qualities that support this, such as speaking loudly, pushing your way in, calling attention to yourself by demanding help, etc.

Go to a place where there are lots of people – a grocery store, an elevator, etc. Embody the pattern fully, infusing your expression with the qualities you identified while playing out the objective. Observe yourself.

How did it feel to embody that pattern? What did you notice about yourself?

Now you might want to try the opposite of the aggressive pattern — shy and withdrawn. *For example,* your objective might be *To Remain Invisible.* Supporting qualities might be silence, shrinking away from others, not asking anyone for anything, etc.

Go to another location and embody the pattern, objective and qualities. Again, observe yourself.

How did it feel to embody the reverse pattern? What did you notice about yourself?

Persons who function in lesser degrees of consciousness are not focused on the individualizing process or on transforming themselves. They don't work on creating new characterizations, let alone know that they are not the predominant character they are creating. Such persons fit all of life into their own character expression.

*For example,* a preacher might preach to his family just as he does to his congregation, or a person who holds values on being strong in every situation will not acknowledge fear even when he feels it. When people do this, they are forcing the circumstances to fit their accustomed way of expressing rather than allowing new facets of self to emerge so that they grow and change as life-artists.

When you live true to your inner spirit, you are registering energy frequencies and you are open to change all the time. But if you live only in your familiar character, you are stuck in your own picture of who you think you are and you are very concerned about how others see you. You not only repeat characteristics with which you feel comfortable, you might go further and take on the behavior of others so that they will feel more comfortable with you. You give up any spontaneous responses in order to hold yourself fixed in the familiar. This is akin to dying a little every day.

If you want to create who you are in every moment consciously, you must be present to what is transpiring, experience it, allow a response to be born in the moment, and choose to give it full expression. This allows you to adapt and to interact with life with freshness and no expectations.

### *Exercise:*

Try actively adapting the next time you are with anyone. Hold an objective that enables you to shift and change in the moment. Discover who you are with each new choice.

### *Exercise:*

It is time for you to decide who your three faces of character will be for your major project. Give them names. Describe the context in which they are most often present. Describe them with characteristics, values, and patterned ways of functioning. Choose a primary objective for each face.

*Here is an example of what I might choose.*

**#1 face: Sports Nut.** She is a persistent force every day, encouraging me to stretch, exercise, swim, and play tennis. She is bouncy, eager, always ready to move, sometimes fanatical about exercising, and willing to push beyond limits. She values moving the body and can't really understand people who are couch potatoes. A patterned way of functioning is that she goes forward with her planned activities without paying attention to inclement weather or her current body condition. A primary objective for her is to continue moving at any cost.

**#2 face: Ms. Outspoken.** She says what is on her mind without weighing how another might receive it or respond to it. She offers what she sees because she values that practice as a duty. She speaks clearly and often metaphorically, inviting others to listen and grow. She is not afraid that others might see her as intrusive. Her mission and primary objective is to speak truth as she sees it. She is committed to that way of living.

**#3 face: The Stand-up Comic.** She has a great sense of humor and adores having fun. She is quick on her feet, able to deliver funny lines with perfect timing. She is more than a jokester; she is a humorist. She values viewing life very lightly and steering people away from self-imposed misery. One of the patterns relating to this lifestyle is that she might blurt out a line that could be inappropriate in the situation. It sounded funny in her own head, so out it comes ready or not. Most of the time, she is very successful and has people around her delighting in her amusing ways. She enjoys being the humorous center of attention. Her objective is to bring levity to the world, to make people laugh.

Once you have determined your three faces, answer these questions: Do these characters slip out of their chosen objectives when others want something else from them? Do they give themselves up in deference to another's needs or wishes?

## Scene Four
## *Practicing Adaptation and Self-Expression*

There are three phases to any interaction with another.

*First:* Putting self forth in an initial thrust

*Second:* Taking into self what the other is putting out

*Third:* Adapting by allowing yourself to be aware of the undercurrent of feeling, and continuing the interaction while giving life to the new that is emerging as a result of what is awakened by the other, even if the qualities you call forth are "uncharacteristic" for you

When you adapt in this way, you make yourself vulnerable to yourself. Not so much to the other, but to the new feelings rising up in you. You have a fresh opportunity to connect with your own inner flow and to give life to it in the now moment. This gives you more range of self-expression and therefore more range of impact and reality creation.

If you try this practice with people in your life

you will discover that it takes a lot of energy to be conscious in an interaction. You really have to be there. You have to make choices. You have to add life force to your expressions of self. This is why so many people prefer to let patterns take over. They can be in an interaction without really being there.

In addition to practicing adaptation, you also want to practice different modes of expression so that you can expand your repertoire.

### *Exercise:*

One way to do this is to choose a nursery rhyme that you know by heart and deliver it in front of a mirror. Make note of the gestures you use and listen to the vocal quality you give to it.

Then do the same nursery rhyme through each of your three faces. Watch for the differences in your delivery and give them full life. Hopefully you will discover that four different "people" performed the same rhyme, putting the emphasis in different places, using different voices and tempo-rhythms, and presenting self in four different ways.

An experience like this serves to stretch you out of your familiar ways of living.

### *Exercise:*

To become more acquainted with each face, take the time to write a soliloquy for each. Focus on an issue, or a problem, or a growing edge that you are dealing with in this face.

## Act Five: On What Instrument?

After you write these three, speak them out loud to yourself, embodying each face while learning about each face.

There are shadow aspects to discover in these three faces. You don't ordinarily give them full life because you have convinced yourself that others won't approve of them. The truth is that somewhere inside yourself, you don't approve of them.

Let them speak. Hear them. Learn about yourself from them.

## Scene Five
# Conscious Characterization

Your characteristic gestures, speech patterns, and the like are not your very own in a personal way. They are generalized ways of functioning in the world. Individuals borrow these cliché mannerisms for daily use when they are functioning under the influence of patterns rather than making the effort to create fresh expressions in the moment. It is your character who lives in these patterns.

You, Player, have the capacity to create the artistic new in every moment. It is possible to get through life playing a passable person in general terms. The patterned clichés do present a portrait of life and the essence of being human. What is missing is individualization, originality, creation, and emergence in the moment.

When the outer character you create is a true image of what the inner spirit is evoking, a finer degree of confidence is achieved. It differs from the self-confidence on the character level which is born of familiarity with ways of being or employment of traits. This confidence is the knowing that comes of inner and outer alignment and it enables you to function creatively even when there is nothing familiar present.

## Act Five: On What Instrument? 221

When functioning through character with this kind of confidence, it is as if you are standing back and observing your character have an interaction with another. Both you and the other are observing the facsimile of self that is representing you.

Knowing yourself to be the creator of the representation, you have total freedom to give life to all traits and actions, including those you hold most intimate (when you are identifying with/as character) and including those you shy away from as lesser or unacceptable.

If you consciously produce a character, you are able to speak and do what you might never dare otherwise. Conscious characterization is a form of reincarnation without needing to die and come in again in a new vehicle. Approach the creative process as if you are incarnating into the new part you are playing in the now moment. Do not waste time producing copies of yourself — hackneyed clichés of overplayed ways of functioning.

Through the nursery rhyme and the soliloquy you had opportunities to get to know a little more about each of your three faces. You have begun to play these faces consciously.

### *Exercise:*

Take a next step. First, find an objective for each face, one that serves your larger purpose in this time period in your life. You want to uncover the more of who the face is rather than play an unconscious version of it. You want to use your creative vehicle to express the faces more fully in movement, voice, speech, gestures, etc.

Consciously move into one of these faces when you make a phone call to a stranger, or when you buy a movie ticket, go shopping, or fill your car. Every time you do this you will come to know more about the face and you will expand your ability to consciously embody the characteristics and objectives that belong to the face.

## Scene Six
## *Fluidity of Motion*

The vital life force, the energy that moves through us, is heated by feeling, emotion, and passion. It is charged by the will and directed by the consciousness of Player. When this is in place the energy moves on the throughline with confidence. It manifests itself in action and is supported by purpose and active objectives. When this flow of energy is in alignment, it is directed by spiritual impulses, by intuition, and by the greater meaning that guides our individual lives.

Once set in motion the energy flows through our muscles and stirs us to create external expression and activity. It invites us to gesture and move in ways that are unique, original, and born in the moment.

Plasticity of motion can be very subtle. If you can, rent the video of *Talking Heads* and watch the brilliant Maggie Smith speak a soliloquy in which, while she tells a story, she exquisitely reveals herself as the teller of that story even though all we see is her head.

Time is essential in plasticity of motion. Most of us do not take a split second of time between movements. When we walk, for example, we are already on the opposite foot going in a forward direction before we have completely finished with the last step. Our walking is therefore held earthbound, rather than soaring. If we would take the split second up on the toes of the finishing step, there would be a split second of flight before the next landing and push off. Try this.

The rise you seek comes in going forward in a horizontal line rather than trying to rise up. There is no interruption in the split second; there is recognition of the momentum. The energy moves up in the spinal column, then down again into the toes in readiness, all the while rotating the hips.

If you can master this split second of flight you will experience your limitless potential through the lift, and a sense of exhilaration will fill you.

Art is born when an unbroken creative line exists. Music is an art form while separate sounds are not. Design is an art form while dots are not. The artist can take the points of separation and carry them along a line of consciousness, creating an unbroken whole: an Art.

### *Exercise:*

Put on music with a good beat and rhythm. Get out into the middle of the floor and imagine that mercury is being poured into the top of your head. Allow it to course down the whole of your body. Let each part of your body become mercurial in its movement as the mercury arrives there, adding one part to the next until the whole body is mercurial as it moves across the room.

## Act Five: On What Instrument? 225

Knowledge of tempo-rhythm leads to chemical balance and to the good health of all the facets of self in their unified expression. Tempo-rhythm is a stimulus to emotional memory and therefore to deep inner experience, or registry, of the Self. True tempo-rhythm is discovered through expression of feelings. Together, the two enable you to touch into your inner motivating forces.

### *Exercise:*

Walk around the room focused on discovering your particular tempo-rhythm. Begin to clap it out with your hands so you can hear it as well as feel and experience it.

Because this tempo-rhythm connects with how you motivate yourself, try some experiments to see if you can maintain it in the midst of contrasting tempo-rhythms. For example, you can put on music that is slower or faster than your natural tempo-rhythm, and sustain your own as a counter-balance.

There will be times in your life when your tempo-rhythm will change or will need to be changed because it is no longer motivating you, no longer in harmony with the greater potential you are now ready to fill. When this occurs, try out new tempo-rhythms to see if something other more closely matches what is calling to you from within. You can do this with music, or you can go out in the world to a busy place where you can watch others walking. As the people go past you, try on their walk, their tempo-rhythm, to see if that links up with the change burgeoning in you.

In all that you do through movement, be conscious of the inner energy moving through you and the feelings that accompany it.

Action that is carried out through movement is inherent in life. The movement is regulated by tempo and the tempo is given its shape by rhythm. This is also true in your speech. Rhythm is given life in syllables that are accented and vowels that are elongated. Return to your soliloquies and read each one aloud, listening for the differences in tempo-rhythm from one face to the next. Add movement to each and you will get a clearer picture of who resides behind this face.

Now that you have returned to each face, remind yourself of your life purpose as you have identified it thus far. Then, identify the primary purpose each face holds for itself. Take a look to see how the three purposes match up with your own overall life purpose. Do they support or detract? Look at the primary characteristics of this face. Do they support or detract? This kind of assessment will enable you to make conscious choices about whether and how you allow these faces to influence you or use any of your life force.

## Scene Seven
## *Restraint and Modulation*

From restraint and modulation of the instrument comes power. I am not speaking here of restricting and limiting, but rather of choosing, directing, and honing.

When you engage in an interaction, all excess gestures are like unwanted lines or scribbles on a canvas. You cannot infuse a presentation with specific and strong movements if you surround yourself with what amounts to clutter. Unrestrained movements make the design you are expressing through your character unclear, monotonous, uncontrolled, and often a blur. Conserve your energy and your forces and direct them specifically and consciously into communicating the inner life you are registering. Excess obscures and dilutes.

A handful of carefully chosen gestures, expressions of movement, evoked from the inner spirit produce a physical action which serves as an unbroken line of communication. Excess tension is akin to static. It interferes with the creative process, as do excess words. All excess robs you of energy. Direct your life force to heighten the essence of what is being communicated. Less is more.

There is a fabulous snippet of a scene in the film *The Dresser*. Albert Finney, playing a great classical actor, is leading his troop through a train station. He is up on a ramp and sees that their train is pulling out of the station. He directs his cane toward the train in one swift, clean gesture, and shouts, "Stop That Train!" emphasizing each of the three words. The train stops and so do we because of the power he so simply directs.

You can practice this by choosing poems and reading them aloud, modulating your delivery and carefully choosing the emphasis on the words.

To move further away from your standard-brand character representation of self, eliminate all unconsciously repeated gestures. These keep you from knowing yourself as Player because they constantly call your attention to self as character.

You are the artist who focuses on purpose and objectives and brings expression to life through movement, voice, speech, and feelings. All this gives you power. When you discover the importance of single gestures, of single movements aligned with inner spirit and directed consciously, you come to know how very powerful you truly can be.

Try all of this in everyday conversation. And, work with restraint and modulation as you once again perform your soliloquies.

## Scene Eight
# Speech and Diction

Speech should not be a string of flat words bouncing off the listener. Speech is at its best when it is poetic or musical. We can create a melody line within self on which we communicate with others while communicating with ourselves. If you are able to create a rhythm in which to function, you will draw others into it as you speak. If what you say is born of your inner spirit you will hear your own soul speaking to you as you speak, and those to whom you speak will enter that same realm with you.

Through pauses, accents, short stops, placement of pauses, etc., it is possible to say the same words many different ways. Practice with such re-phrasing enables you to hear afresh what you are saying and to truly identify what you are saying. The sound of your own voice is speaking to you before it ever speaks to anyone else.

### Exercise:

Take the phrases, *I must have love to live,* or *I will remain conscious if I have purpose*, or *Do not say that to me*. Play with all three of these, placing the emphasis, accent, and pause in different places. Sense the changing meaning. See if you can identify in what inner place in yourself the variations are registered. They might touch your heart center, or your solar plexus, or get you moving to action in your generative center.

Every time you underscore a word or single it out as important in a phrase or sentence, you are pointing to the core of what you are saying. You are offering the inner essence of your being. Listen to what you are communicating from yourself to yourself. Focus on transmitting what you are registering. Let others see what you are saying. Speak to the eyes of others, to their souls rather than to their ears. Speak from your heart to their hearts. You are not simply communicating information, you are touching others with your depth of knowing and with your feelings.

It is not only true that sentences and words convey meaning but also that each syllable does and that if you want to be functioning as a life-artist, you need to know the impact you make on your world with each syllable, each vowel, and each consonant. Every one of them carries an energy impact. Trained actors know this very well, and you also need to know it as a life-artist.

There are sentences that are delivered in such a powerful way that they live on seemingly forever. Think of President Franklin D. Roosevelt saying over the airwaves, "The only thing we have to fear is fear itself." There was a rising inflection on that first word fear and it hung in the air creating suspense about what the answer would be. Then it came,

## Act Five: On What Instrument?

with full force, "fear itself," with a stress on itself.

Or think of Clark Gable in *Gone with the Wind:* "Frankly, my dear, I don't give a damn." There was such freedom in him, such release, that she was completely dismissed and left standing in the emptiness of her life.

The very way you speak may push others away while you seek to draw them in. If you mumble or do not project, another will stain to hear for a while but will soon quit listening. Sloppy speaking muddles what is being communicated. If words are not chosen carefully and spoken clearly, they tend to conceal meaning and detract from the essence rather than express what is fully intended.

Your manner of speaking is one of the fastest routes to harmony and union, and equally, one of the easiest ways to offend and cause separation.

Human beings came to language instinctively, through impulses. They didn't invent it in their heads. We are spoken to by the natural world and our words are symbols of the sounds that influence us.

### *Exercise:*

Now return to your work with creating three faces of self. When you work with your soliloquies for each of your faces remember to communicate with yourself and then through yourself to others. Say the words of the soliloquy for each face and pay particular attention to the speech, the diction, the pauses, and to the gestures and movements you choose.

In all of your work with these three faces, these three predominant aspects of yourself, always ask yourself as you proceed, what am I learning about myself from communicating with myself through this face?

## Scene Nine
# Intonations, Tempos, and Functioning Consciously

Most people pay little or no attention to their ways of speaking. They are supported in this in ordinary life because they are accustomed to hearing the same carelessness in others. If you choose to create your life character consciously, you have to guide and direct yourself to see, to walk, to move, to speak, and to engage with others. This is what an actor must do. He can't just 'be' on the stage. He must consciously occupy space on the stage because everything he does communicates something important to the audience and everything he does contributes to the unfolding of the play.

Now just imagine if you thought of your daily life that way. Everything you do communicates something important to another person. Not only that, it actually imprints the whole of unfolding life. And everything you do contributes to that unfolding. It is almost overwhelming to realize how much consciousness this requires and what a different world this might be if everyone functioned this way!

Words and the way they are spoken are far more important in conscious life than in ordinary life. In conscious life you must speak the text of Player (which functions as an inner playwright). In ordinary life you tend to say things so often and in so patterned a way that your speech could easily become mechanical and devoid of inner essence. You tend to live much like cliché actors who don't believe a word of what they are saying, who speak without living the content of what the author has written, who don't truly listen when they are spoken to by another character in the scene, and who wait only to deliver their own lines, often interrupting before their cue.

You need to realize that you are creating life as you are living it. You don't just open your mouth and emit sounds, not if you want to function as Player and live consciously.

## *Exercise:*

Try the following. Close your eyes and groan and moo into what we call the mask, the resonating chambers in your face on both sides of your nose and in the middle of your forehead. Feel the vibration, first with your lips closed, then with them open. Breathe into the center of your body (not lifting your shoulders but feeling the diaphragm push your abdomen outward and retreat when you use the breath to make sound.) Tip your head forward and drop your chin. This facilitates emitting the sound as far forward as possible. See if you can feel the open notes (oohs and ahhs) supporting themselves in the opening of the hard palate and reverberating in the nasal cavities and the closed notes

## Act Five: On What Instrument? 235

(ehhs and ihhs) supported in the nasal cavities and reverberating against the hard palate.

The inside of the head is a master instrument of resonance. Use the making of sound as a probe to discover different inner points of reverberation and the alternating qualities of sound that emerge. You might not be used to working with your mouth and opening it. Practice yawning and moving your jaw. This will release tension and it allows the throat and mouth to expand so that sounds can be made more easily.

## *Exercise:*

One of the main elements of making full and clear sound is being conscious of creating an unbroken line. You want to have a flow of sound, as if you were singing. Choose a song and sing it to remind yourself of the flow. Now pick up one of your poems and sing it. Alternate with speaking it to see if you can sustain the flow. Make room for all the sounds, both the vowels and the consonants. Then try all of this in everyday conversation, making sure there is resonance and flow.

Stretch yourself by listening, in unfamiliar environments, to the accents and dialects of others. See if you can speak English the way they do, utilizing different intonations, and different pronunciations. If you are unfamiliar with how Spanish speakers roll their "r" sound, try it. Make the tip of your tongue vibrate against the front of your upper palate. If you do this with many different accents and dialects you will stretch yourself beyond your own comfort zone and open yourself to character expressions you never knew were possible.

Too many of us live in one place and speak like everyone around us. Then we call all others "foreigners" or "aliens" because we forget that we are one being with multiple expressions.

I have traveled to over 65 countries. I can always make my way if I encounter someone with limited English because when I speak with them, I convert my English to their accent and they can more readily understand me. I have mastered accents and dialects for Spanish, English, French, British, Indian, Egyptian, German, New York, Maine, the Carolinas, the Mid West, etc. And every time I shift into English with another accent, I can feel the change in my tempo-rhythm, in my intonation, in the way I pause, and even in my facial expressions. It is extremely liberating. I can be at home anywhere. I can become whoever is in front of me.

Because I can so easily shift my character into different expressions, I am less bothered by people who are very different from my normal ways of being. I "try on" how they do life and suddenly it is not foreign.

This also makes it easier for me to remain centered in the midst of very different ways of being so that I don't lose who I am. A way to practice this is to put on music I find jangling and stay true to myself through a series of tasks, never losing my own tempo-rhythm. This is important practice for staying true to self in the midst of any chaotic scene.

## Act Five: On What Instrument?

*Exercise:*
This might be a good time to use your nursery rhyme or a poem and try speaking it in various accents or dialects. Listen to how it changes with each reading.

There are moments when you might want to present something on the outside that is quite different from what you are feeling on the inside. If you do this consciously, you are creating two different tempo-rhythms simultaneously. You might be seething with anger within but present an utterly calm demeanor on the outside. If you have a purpose for doing this, and you do it consciously, you can live in both worlds at once and not have any feelings left over because you have chosen to do this consciously. Life is like a complicated piece of music which has varying and often contradictory patterns coexisting.

You can maintain balance in the midst of contradiction.

## Scene Ten
## *Making an Imprint*

Constantin Stanislavski reported:

> Nature has so arranged matters that when we are in verbal communication with others, we first see the word on the retina of the mind's eye and then we speak of what we have thus seen. If we are listening to others we first take in through the ear what they are saying and then we make the mental picture of what we have heard.
>
> To hear is to see what is spoken of, to speak is to draw visual images.
>
> To an actor a word is not just a sound, it is the evocation of images. So when you are in verbal intercourse on the stage, speak not so much to the ear as to the eye.[1]

In life, everything we say is more enlivened and our communication is enriched when we choose words to speak that evoke images. This is easier to do if we touch our feelings as we speak because

---
1 *Building a Character,* page 113.

## Act Five: On What Instrument?

feelings add texture to our words.

If you watch daytime TV talk shows you know that you are most interested when the interviewee shares personal experiences and fills the telling of them with feeling. For contrast, think of sitting in a lecture hall hearing a professor read the same instructional notes he has delivered for years. In the lecture hall, it is easy to go to sleep. Watching the talk show we are not only touched but we feel as if we are participating.

If you are going to communicate, fill your words with energy and passion.

Every time you speak, the intonation you choose has an effect on your emotions, your memory, your feelings, your thoughts, and to the same degree on others. What you say and what you don't say carries an impact. There is palpable power in eloquent silences that are well chosen. These silences cause the words that had been spoken to swell. They enable the speaker to send forth scarcely perceptible rays of light/energy. They impregnate the words that are yet to come.

### *Exercise:*

Try this with a friend. Close your eyes, breathe deeply, and touch something in your life about which you are feeling deeply or passionately. Write a paragraph using carefully chosen words and images to powerfully convey the depth, the passion, the burning concern. Read it to yourself choosing where to pause and what intonation will most effectively communicate the heat of the subject matter.

Next, deliver it to your friend.

Then release any tension you might have. Relax the muscles of your speaking apparatus. Do not focus on volume or "playing" the passion. Deliver it once more from the relaxed state but bringing in what worked in the first presentation. The impact you will make with this reading will be significant but without any forcing.

Ask your friend what impact both readings made.

## Scene Eleven
## Subtext

What is it that lies underneath and behind the actual words you speak? The subtext is the inner world of energy, traveling on the throughline, that flows uninterrupted beneath what you are speaking. That energy gives those words life and a basis for existing. The subtext is made up of varied patterns inside all that you say. It is born of frequencies you register which are then made manifest through your words and actions. It is motivated by and is offered in response to the given circumstances of the moment. You give it all life through your imagination. You are not aware of any of this as you are living your life. Yet, these intentionally interwoven elements run all through your life play and eventually lead to the unknowable Super-Objective.

In a written play there is a similar sub-textual stream. Actors tap into it and, through their actions and speech, make it manifest so that an audience can sense it.

You could call all of the above, speaking with soul. Soul is always accompanied by feeling. When you speak you should bear in mind on some level that you are using words to allow others to touch the frequency you are registering. As your interaction proceeds, you will arouse feelings in the other person, as well as images and sensorial responses.

As soon as a life-artist breathes life into the subtext of what is to be conveyed to another, a form of merging is achieved. The essence of the speaker combines with the essence of the listener and something larger than the two individuals takes form. This is the real art of conversation. It is an act of creation. It is as if the life-artist is composing and singing the music of his feelings. According to Stanislavski, "When we hear the melody of a living soul we then, and only then, can come to a full appreciation of the worth and beauty of the lines and all they hold concealed."[2]

Listen to yourself throughout the day. All too often you toss words about. They clutter the environment rather than creating word pictures that evoke sensual images. If you want to function more consciously, care must be taken in the selection of words so that you too can tap the subtext.

## *Exercise:*

Do a page of inner stream of consciousness writing for each of your three faces. Allow the poetry of the soul of the face to emerge. Read it aloud to yourself when you finish. Allow yourself to be imprinted by what you are saying to yourself and what you are discovering about each face.

---

2 *Op. Cit.,* page 110.

There is a spiritual law: as above, so below. You are practicing this through the creation of the three faces. The unseen creative force in the universe (some call it God) breathed out through sound to make form. In the beginning there was the word. Everything that is is of this creative force. It is; we are.

Everything is the outpouring of this creative force, both inanimate and animate. If you want to have a picture of what some call God, travel the planet and the whole universe to see all the different manifestations because God is all of those. Everything, everyone is what we call God. Manifestation occurs in order to know Self experientially. God made everything manifest to know Itself.

Everything you do, every action, every word you speak, is part of Self discovering Self. We label some things good or bad, yet it is all part of the whole. It is the creative force in action, as above, so below.

What you are doing in the creation of these three faces is breathing out, giving voice and form to what was hidden. It was lurking in you but was not fully manifested so you couldn't see it. You are creating the three faces in order to know Self.

I like to define God as continuously unfolding perfection. Its knowledge is gained through experience, embodiment, and observation. This leads to continuous refinement.

As you create the three faces you experience and choose what to keep, what to release, and what to further develop. This process can be called the evolution of the Self.

## Scene Twelve
## *A Principled Approach to Theatre*

One of the most useful statements Stanislavski made during his years of teaching was, "Love art in yourself and not yourself in art."

He was speaking about more than refraining from being ego-invested. He was advising against too much focus on success which by definition is fleeting. What he held as most important was creativity and all its secrets.

This is vital in your daily life as well. Life should be treated as holy. Every time you make an entrance, that is, begin a day, you need to remember that life is a holy sanctuary and come to it with consciousness and purpose. Anything that detracts should be released.

Every time you enter a human dynamic in the theatre of life, you are there to serve the art form of conscious living. When you do this you function not just as an individual but collectively in an ensemble of humanity that is the manifestation of the creative force.

Your life is an on-going rehearsal during which you align with what is being asked of you and cen-

## Act Five: On What Instrument?

ter yourself to creatively make it a reality. In this way, your attention is on exquisite creativity rather than mere survival.

Singers vocalize every day. Dancers keep muscles in shape at the bar. Musicians play scales. Writers write something every day. To quote Stanislavski, "A day omitted is a day lost and a detriment to the art of the performer." Every day your task as a life-artist is "... to cultivate the most delicate and precise ways of rendering all the subtle intricacies of human thoughts and feelings, visual observations and emotional impressions."[3]

You don't ever stop rehearsing. You don't ever graduate from this discipline. It lasts your whole life and is even more important as you age.

Never become a consciousness drone who waits around to be led along the path, or who must watch others to become infused with creative fire, or who needs constantly to be pushed away from dead center. Such drones lean on the creative work of others. They are a drag on the accomplishments of everyone.

The task for each of us is to give form to the inner life registered by Player through the character, expressing that life in dynamic terms. Our work is to embody what we know, lest we become a windbag of concepts.

This is a perfect time to take this work a step further.

---

3 *Op. cit.*, page 252.

## Exercise:

Gather some friends with whom you can interact while embodying each face. You will need to set the scene for each improvisation. Where are you? Who are you? What is your objective (what do you want in this interaction)? When does this take place? Why is this taking place? What just happened in the moment before this scene is occurring?

Do an improvisation with one friend for each face. Tell the other person who he (or she) is in relation to you and set up the scene so that there will be conflict between the two of you. Make sure you give the other person a strong objective to play.

The purpose of the improvisation is to experience this face in interaction, in relationship. Each face should have a different circumstance, a different objective and different ways of achieving that objective (activities). The objective is: what do you want? The activities are: what do you do to get what you want? And when there is dramatic conflict, you have a stimulating obstacle that stands in the way of what you want. You use as many activities as possible to navigate past the obstacle and achieve your objective. Here is where the particular use of speech, diction, pauses, gestures, and all the rest comes into play.

## Exercise:

When you have completed the three improvisations, make notes of what you discovered in the interactions. What happens when the face interacts with another as differentiated from talking to self, through the face, in a soliloquy? Look at the characteristics you brought to life. What will you release? What do you need to introduce to make this face more effective? What new actions can you take and in relation to whom?

## Scene Thirteen
# Patterns of Accomplishment

Here are some reminders for you as a life-artist about the creative process in which you are engaged.

There is a trinity in creative work: head-center (crown chakra) registry, will, and feelings.

The creative process begins with head-center registry: an imaginative interaction with your inner world. It is brought into consciousness on the throughline from the unformed into expression. The creative process must then be taken one step at a time through units and objectives which give easier access to action.

By concentrating on all that is around you in your immediate environment, your chosen objectives will be more grounded and more easily fulfilled.

Always function from a sense of truth and your objectives will be infused with power. You will not fall into unconscious, patterned living (which is really dull and lifeless existence).

Infuse yourself with energy so that you are filled with passion and desire to do all your actions fully. Those actions will lead to communion with self

## Act Five: On What Instrument? 249

and with others. Remember when you are communing and merging with others, you want to adapt not accommodate.

Move your body while being conscious of your inner tempo-rhythm and make every movement and gesture a meaningful act so that it carries power and imprints everyone around you.

Touch your feelings and give them full life. When you do this you will touch others and you will allow yourself to be touched by others. This leads to union.

Only at the end of this process do you want to evaluate and journey to your mind to think about what has just occurred. Don't spend too much time there because you want to begin again with registry and with activating the creative process.

All of the above requires that you be fully present in every moment. You need to have creative jurisdiction over the self. You can practice this by doing an exercise with your physical body.

### *Exercise:*

Relax fully, slowly letting go of sections of your body. Let the body sink to the floor. Observe it in this perfectly still state.

After a short while, deliberately begin to awaken the various parts of your body by stretching, limbering, lifting, and moving. Rise to your feet and feel the circulation activated.

Now awaken your voice, sending it clearly and with resonance through the mask and feeling the vibrations. Throw the tones out fully enough to feel them come back to you from the walls and furniture.

Now speak a line or two with sharp diction and good volume that communicates the power of your being as you register within and give what you register expression.

Move your body into cycles of rhythm, both standing in place and swaying in different rhythms.

Now that the instrument is limbered, breathe into a strong urge to move, to do some action, to fulfill and express the spirit within you. You are poised and ready but before you move, give yourself a strong objective. Know what you want and give it life. Act on it with passionate energy. This state of readiness in the body is the external creative state.

You are in charge of this instrument. You give it life. You move it. You use it as a vehicle of expression. It is moved by your will. When you have developed creative jurisdiction and your vehicle is ready and able to serve you, the inner and outer creative states meet. You are poised and ready with your physical capacities and inner resources for a merging, a meeting of you with the life moment. Unless you are in this state, you cannot give yourself fully to the experience of bringing into being what you know.

## Scene Fourteen
## *The Natural Laws of Living*

We are born with an innate capacity for creativity. Yet we have inflicted ourselves with the malady of forced, untruthful, conventional living. We do not act naturally and thus creatively. Instead, we perform contortions of pretentious proportions. We seek to manufacture creativeness rather than knowing that creativity is an active part of us and does not require insincere or trumped up representation. On the stage of life, all we need to do is live in accordance with natural laws. We discover these by opening to listen and yielding to what we hear in our inner selves. Nothing about the process is complicated.

**The Theatre of Life** is an organic approach to re-entering the world of natural law. It is a way of life that must be assimilated until it becomes a way of being. It is studied in parts and then merged into a whole so that it can be understood in all its fundamentals. When you have seen all the parts you can have a true grasp of its entirety, as with the natural creative state itself.

This way of life needs to be lived daily in order that the life-artist can become aligned with functioning according to the true dictates of his/her inner self.

The character, often has no awareness of techniques, no means of awakening feelings, no knowledge of his/her nature, and little way of getting back onto the right path once he/she has strayed, because there is no way to activate consciousness.

You, however, as a life-artist have creative faculties available to you when you function consciously. You can access your intuition if you are present to yourself. You can function with purpose and give expression to what you know. Creating an artful life is a full time job. It is Player's job; character is the instrument through which everything is expressed and experienced.

# ACT SIX

# I AM

*Preparation for
Creating a Life Role*

"After stifling self-expression all my life, I discover that full expression provides full experience, and full experience requires full expression. I have learned that absolutely everything is part of the Whole. All is usable; everything that happens serves multiple purposes."

— Hollis Johnson, San Diego, CA

"I feel reborn into an entirely difference sense of self. My character is now expandable and flexible, not set in concrete. I can embody the characteristics I choose and withdraw energy from aspects of character that no longer serve."

— Joan Kerber, Chagrin Falls, OH

"I am a totally different person. I have a sense of purpose now that has been lacking in my life. I sense where to go. Before, I was foundering in good intentions."

— Diana Farquharson, Belleville, ON

"I must be true to Self. I cannot afford to poison my psyche with accommodation. I cannot bend to the hypnotic lure of external acceptance. The poison invades slowly at first, then races through my being, cutting my connection to what is sensitive and nurtures me: my Self."

— Mary Ann McCarthy, San Francisco, CA

"I can merge Player and character more seamlessly in any scene by choosing and calling forth qualities, and by focusing on objectives that are from the heart."

— Margarite Bradley, Flagstaff, AZ

"I leave clothed with purposes and objectives, myriads of resources, skills, learnings, insights, and inspiration. Clothed in these garments I will be at home anywhere, with anyone. I am dressed for each exciting, full moment."

— Suzanne Himmelwright, Belvedere, CA

"The result of **Theatre of Life** work is a palpable, growing sense of inner union, and a connection through the heart with all that is. Since starting this work I have had many experiences of being on the throughline both spontaneously and intentionally, and it feels powerful, satisfying and connecting."

— Don Woodside, Hamilton, ON

## Scene One
## *Preparation*

Take some time to assess the work you have done thus far as you have made your way through the preceding Acts.

### *Exercise:*
What major shifts in your sense of self and your character functioning are you aware of as you look back over your life since Act I?

Here is a thought-provoking quotation from the French philosopher Gaston Berger:

> Am I now able to answer the question which I was asking at the beginning of my inquiry? Can I say who am I? Nothing could be less sure. I have learned to recognize in the personality more or less profound levels. I have taken back properties to their own principles. But levels cover

a center, and properties have an owner. I have pushed as far as possible my investigation without ever being able to get at something more than my belonging. To recognize them as mine, means to differentiate myself from them. I certainly am not either this body through which sensations come, and which I use for action, nor those tendencies, good or bad ones, that manifest through it. I can even see in the light of experience that I cannot be a body or an aggregate of bodies or a characteristic derived from some particular form of bodies. Those hypotheses which I am refusing were not false propositions, but meaningless affirmations. However even if I cannot in any way get hold of myself, I nevertheless know that I am, and that I cannot doubt to be . . . If I wanted to speak more rigorously, I should then say I am I, expressing in this unusual way the fact that the I is always the subject. If I prefer to use a term which belongs both to common use and to the philosopher's language, I will not say, as is sometimes done, that I have a soul (which, to be precise, is contradictory), but that I am a soul. [Source unknown.]

## *Exercise:*

What statement can you make now about the question with which we began this work: "Who AM I?"

## Act Six: I Am

In Act Six your continuous preparation will be your attunement in energy: (a) aligning your consciousness on the throughline as character and Player, and (b) opening to the larger pattern in which we are all functioning and asking guidance, help, insight, and direction from The Source, or whatever you call it. It will serve you to open to the More, the Whole, in which you are integrated.

Here is a wonderful quote from Sri Aurobindo's epic poem *Savitri*:

> For centuries you have waited for this time. Now it has come: the hour of the Unexpected; the Hour of God . . . when the Spirit moves among men and the breath of the Lord is abroad upon the waters of your being . . . when even a little effort changes destiny.
> I see . . . the Omnipotent's flaming pioneers come crowding down the amber stairs of births; forerunners of a divine multitude . . .
> I see them . . . cross the twilight of an age, the sun eyed children of a marvelous dawn, the massive barrier-breakers of the world, carrying the magical word, the mystic fire . . . Swimmers of Love's laughing fiery floods and dancers within rapture's golden doors . . .

Using this quote as inspiration, I would like you to focus now on this breakdown of purposes and objectives for your work in Act Six.

## Purposes:

- To foster, nourish and sustain the individualizing process
- To orient, guide and support the character-self during its process of transformation
- To come to know through experience that you are a creative life-artist
- To open more fully to the source of creativity within, and to allow the free flow of energy from that source
- To learn skills for the conscious living of a creative life
- To integrate all the facets of self on one throughline of energy
- To learn to activate characteristics supportive of your purposes and objectives in each life moment
- To enjoy association with others seeking creative excellence in the individualizing process

**Objectives** *(which could also be considered purposes for each preceding Act of the* **Theatre of Life** *work):*

## Act Six: I Am

- Act One: To come to know who I am
- Act Two: To discover how to create a useful environment for becoming
- Act Three: To learn to direct energies in order to empower both experience and expression on the character level
- Act Four: To create meaning for my character-self by aligning life units and objectives with all-embracing purposes
- Act Five: To discover my uniqueness as a life actor and to hone the instrument of character in order to play life's music more artfully
- Act Six: To stand in the moment before the moment of creation and, in full consciousness, bring my Self into form for truthful experience and creative expression

During this Act you will hopefully come to know yourself as the I AM, without boundaries. You will explore what it means to create your life role consciously. You will recognize the feel/know as the point of merging between character/Player. In order to do this you have to orient yourself in higher frequencies of energy. As you do this you will come closer to awakening your unknown Super-Objective.

All of the above will be facilitated as you express the Will through creative purposes and objectives, recognize and trust the motivating force of creative emotions, and give physical embodiment to the new by "incarnating a role."

Act Six focuses on rehearsal for birthing, for consciously birthing/creating a character through whom you want to function in the world. To rehearse is to prepare. You are in rehearsal for creating a life role and your work is your preparation. Unfolding is never ending. To be finished is death. Upon completion of Act Six, you will be at the next beginning.

## *Exercise:*

As you begin to read and work in Act Six, choose a specific commitment to embody every day and something to abstain from that interferes with your conscious creativity. Write these down and name one specific way to begin to implement each.

For example, you might choose to become aware of and express your feelings at least twice every day; or, to say exactly what you mean every time you speak and eliminate any prefaces or apologies or story-telling; or, to direct your character consciously throughout the day.

Examples of abstaining from patterns which interfere with conscious creativity might be smoking (which clouds your energy field), overeating (which can make you sluggish), worrying (which drains your creative force), etc.

## Scene Two
## Ways of Preparing: Fresh Acquaintance

Who Am I? I AM. I AM Player. Player configurates character through whom you have your being on the stage of life. Knowing Self as Player replaces the quest of character in search of Higher Self.

Something key to hold in your consciousness is: Do not be oppressed by identification with the character. Know yourself as Player who functions through a character you are creating.

To remain identified with Self rather than character, always ask in each life encounter, what *would* I do if I were in this character's situation, not, what *should* I do?

Acknowledge the character's particular life expression in his/her time, city, and circumstance and ask, what would I do if I were that character? Remain the observer in the choice-making position about your expression in the world.

How can you give fullest expression of your feeling/sensing/knowing through this ready, willing, prepared vehicle?

The key words in response to this question are Feel/Know.

Character believes knowing comes from thinking. Knowing actually comes from feeling that is registered and expressed. The action is determined by Player and given expression through character, your vehicle of service to Self. If Player is not functioning consciously, previous patterns are automatically activated.

## *Fresh Acquaintance:*

A practical way of remaining conscious in each moment is to practice making fresh acquaintance with self and others. As you do, you will want to speak truth in order to feel what you know and know what you feel. This will arouse artistic desires and inner aspirations so that you can embody inner urges in external action.

When *Player* meets other persons for the first time, you have a fresh impression. (*Character* doesn't necessarily have this experience because of a backlog of values and attitudes.) In a similar fashion, meet the facets of yourself with fresh acquaintance as they emerge through your character. This first impression will stimulate your artistic enthusiasm and awaken peak energy for the creative process. Each fresh impression is a seed of new potential, not a redo of a previous pattern.

Fresh Acquaintance is unprejudiced. Prejudice is born of your previous opinions which are held recorded in character and keep you bound to history. Fresh acquaintance allows you to have your own relationship with your character, not from its perspective but from yours as Player.

## Act Six: I Am  263

Your character's impression of itself is based on thoughts. Your knowledge of your character is based on feeling. To know is synonymous with to feel. Give expression to what you feel, not to what you think.

### *Exercise:*
Mirrors provide you with a reflection of a reflection. The character reflects a Player directive; the mirror reflects the character's reflection.

Stand in front of a mirror viewing the reflection of a reflection. Remind yourself that you see the image. The image never sees you. Player has the power to view its projection.

Report on what you see freshly in this moment. The new and fresh that you will see depends on who is looking not on what is seen.

You might want to try this with a small group of friends or family members. All of you stand in front of a wide mirror in which all of you are visible to each other. You all begin by closing your eyes and breathing to clear the channels. Upon opening your eyes, you all observe each other in Fresh Acquaintance. Do not look at your own image. See who your eyes settle on.

Each person will say whom he/she is observing in the mirror. A moment ago you saw your character afresh. Now hear afresh what others are saying. If they refer to your character, observe what they are observing as if it were someone else's character in the room. Everyone will be observing what the speaker is observing and this will further freshen your own viewing.

Now, sit your character down in front of the full-length mirror with your eyes closed. Family and friends gather behind to see your character in the mirror at the same time. Breathe deeply and still yourself. With each breath touch what you experience in self right now and allow it to be expressed through your whole self and face, replacing the mask of character that was there a moment ago. When you open your eyes, look into this fresh impression of your character and say aloud all that you see and experience. The group will say what they see. Then all of you will report on the whole experience.

To rehearse for birth into the energy world is a first birth. Rehearsing for birth into Light's Regions is preparation for enlightenment. In this realm there are no images. You see directly, face to face rather than seeing reflected images. Images are but a reflection of the Reality. The Reality is in the feeling, in the consciousness that projects the image. The reflection in the mirror exists because you are the power to project it. You are, therefore you project. You are, therefore you observe.

Fresh Acquaintance comes as a result of being open to all possibilities at all times, acknowledging that all that exists is equal in value. Fresh Acquaintance is to meet the moment without an overlay of past history.

## Scene Three
## *Ways of Preparing: Artistic Analysis*

A second way of working in the period of preparation is Artistic Analysis: becoming aware of what is alive in your character now in order to better know the vehicle through which you function in the world.

I invite you to do a study of your life derived from an examination of the seven major facets of consciousness which correspond to the seven rays of frequencies affecting your unfolding process. The facets you will examine are as follows.

- **The External Facet** (what is observable to others): comprised of the facts of your life, significant events, the form it has taken

- **The Social Facet:** historical setting, nationality, standard of living, style of living

- **The Aesthetic Facet** (choice based on taste): environment, colors, textures, sources of nourishment — the scenery and costuming of your character life

- **The Psychological Facet:** feelings, inner actions, beliefs, ideals
- **The Physical Facet:** body shape, external character traits, habits, choices of action, tempo-rhythm.
- **The Inner Facet** (wherein spiritual truth lives and has its being): intuitions and knowing gained through experience, sense of being's integrity, direct perceptions of the energy world
- **The Mental Facet:** concepts, thoughts, images, memories, longings, reasoning, abstract reflections of values

## *Exercise:*

Flesh out each of these facets with words and phrases that you know to be a valid expression of you. Choose freshly in this moment of acquaintance with self what is true of/for you now.

After you write responses for each facet read them over to gain an overview of how you know yourself.

Upon completion of this Artistic Analysis, ask yourself, if I were not being this character right now, who would I choose and what draws me to this other? Let yourself be drawn to someone, living or dead, as you were drawn in energy in Act Two to a painting.

## Scene Four
# *Ways of Preparing:*
# *External Circumstances*

A third way of working in this period of preparation is to determine the influence of the external circumstances on your life, both past and present. External circumstances include the physical environment in which you grew up, the family that influenced your life, the schooling you had, and the friends with whom you surrounded yourself.

*For example,* I was very influenced by my external circumstances. I grew up in Brooklyn, New York, on a street of apartment buildings with no trees or green anywhere in sight. It was a drab concrete environment with little view of the sky. As a result, I was determined to travel the world, to live amidst flowers, and to have space. Our small two-bedroom apartment housed five of us and I never had a room of my own, a desk, or a creative space of my own.

I was influenced in yet another way. I expanded inside myself. My imagination flowered and soared. I lived with vibrant images, wrote poetry, and expressed in art. If everything had been available to me in the outer, I don't know if I would have developed as significantly on the inner.

I could give you examples of family influences, etc., but you get the idea.

You are influenced by external circumstances. You believe that what is happening to you is real. However, that "reality," and your response to it, is restricted to the moment and time period in which it is occurring.

The reality of my neighborhood was confining and limiting. My response to it then was to make the best of it. I would pull into myself and day-dream of open spaces. A friend who had asthma went to live in the dry climate of Arizona for a while and came back with tantalizing tales of the desert and the sky. I wanted to "get" asthma so I could go to Arizona and live in spaciousness. As I grew older, however, I longed for the ocean and lived in California for 21 years. I wanted to be near water because that became a nourishing factor for me. Oddly enough, I then moved to Arizona!

If I lived in a confined space now, my response might be to delight in the closeness of everything and the ease of accessibility. I might expand out from my inner self to enlarge my personal space.

The effect of the external circumstances changes based on how you interact with them. While the external circumstances appear "real," you are the creator of the reality of how you see them and how you react or respond to them.

## *Exercise:*

Choose three major life circumstances in which external events seemed to affect or cause the course of your feelings and responses. Now choose the one that has the greatest current charge on it. Tell a partner about the circumstance or write about it in your journal. What feelings did it evoke in you? What did you do in response to it, what actions? Give life to the feelings that are evoked through movement and sound.

**Fresh Impressions:** What do you now feel about your past external circumstances after giving the feelings life in this way? What are you feeling now? Make some notes for yourself.

## *Exercise:*

Engage your creative imagination. Envision that you are standing on the apron of the stage (the area in front of the curtain.) Think of it as a crossover line. All that is behind the proscenium arch is the womb of Player in which the whole creative process germinates. You make yourself manifest through character by breaking through the proscenium arch in expression, with the creative force behind you.

In this exercise you will have an opportunity to cross over from the past to the present. You will birth your own feelings in relation to the past and then the present, in relation to a given external circumstance.

**Step one:**
Use the circumstance you previously chose. What feelings were evoked in you then? Stand with your eyes closed at the imaginary crossover line. Behind you, the wind of your previous experience is pushing at the door of your awareness, communicating through you in order that you might re-experience your feelings of the past as evoked by the external event you have chosen. Give the feelings physical expression.

**Step Two:**
Return to your starting position. Turn your attention once again to the circumstance and the feelings. This time feel the call of the new in the form of powerful energy in front of you, pulling you to the now and to new freedom. As you allow yourself to be pulled forward, release what you felt and open yourself to discover what you feel now in relation to that old circumstance and give it physical life. Be aware of what you discover about new choices. Make notes.

Before you depart from Scene Four, make a list of qualities you don't have and don't want, and a list of qualities you don't have and do want.

## Scene Five
# Ways of Preparing: Appraising the Facts

There are certain qualities of Self you wish to retain and others you do not. This is based on preferences you have which stem from values. Values are arbitrary, although systems of right and wrong would tell you what values you should and shouldn't have. Each person, group, and nation . . . adopts values and seeks to impose them on others they say are holding the "wrong" values. Player knows that no value is greater or lesser than any other. Character resists this knowledge in order to have a secure system by which to live. Every single value and act is an expression of the Creative Force.

### Exercise:
Reflect on the following and make notes. Choose one quality you said you didn't want. In whom have you known it? What was the impact on you because this certain someone held that value or embodied that quality? If you were to exhibit it, what is the worst thing that could happen to you, to others?

How can you be actively compassionate in relation to this quality in others or in self without making excuses for it?

Now look at the quality you said you do want: What specific actions can you take to bring this into being? In whom have you seen it exhibited? What has been the impact of it on you or others?

How are these two qualities related? How are they the dark and light of each other? How can one serve the other?

A fourth way of working in this period of preparation is appraising the facts. This is an outer journey to the inner. It relates to the principle, as above, so below; as within, so without.

The inner life, the spiritual life, the life of Player is exhibited in outer circumstances, in the life of the character. If you penetrate the external (Player is looking for itself in the manifested expression of the character) you will uncover the inner essence.

Going from the periphery to the center, from the form to the substance, you inevitably enter the inner life of Self, Player. Appraising the facts is to step inside the character you are playing, as if it were you, and assess the outer in order to break into awareness of the inner pattern. The inner pattern is who you know/feel yourself to be which is then exposed through the facts and actions of the character self.

A stage actor can't approach a role without having some appraisal of the facts of the character, its relationship to other characters, and the place of the character within the play.

I will never forget the actor who did the opposite of this. I attended a presentation at a small theatre in San Diego. The occasion was a talk by the renowned playwright Edward Albee. He spoke to us of many of his characters and their motivations.

In the course of the presentation, as a way of giving back to Mr. Albee, two members of the company did an early scene from Albee's brilliant play, *Who's Afraid of Virginia Woolf?* The characters of George and Martha are in a relationship that is defined by sarcasm and frequent acrimony. Forty-eight-year-old George is more milk-toast than manly as the curtain opens. His fifty-two-year-old wife Martha, daughter of the university president, is disappointed that history-teacher George has aborted his academic career. The actor playing George chose to be extremely assertive and antagonistic in the delivery of his lines. He should have been dominated by Martha.

After they played the scene, Mr. Albee asked the actor why he had played George with such force and vehemence, considering that this side of him is not given any expression until much later in the play. The actor replied (if you can believe this) that he had read only this first scene they were going to perform and had not read the rest of the play.

Those of us who were present hung our heads in heavy embarrassment and astonishment. How could he have not read the rest of the play? How would he dare insult Mr. Albee and the entire craft of acting with this gross omission? By playing George this way in the beginning, the character had no place to go in his development.

Mr. Albee, consummate professional that he is, simply replied, "I see."

We all need to be conscious of the facts of our lives and what has influenced our characters to this point. Then we need to make conscious choices about how we want to proceed.

We lie to ourselves when we speak about ourselves in patterned ways rather than making an assessment in the now moment and saying what is true for us right now as we register it in fresh acquaintance. Instead, we allow the character to assess us. It knows nothing. Character functions with facts, so called, that are derived from empty patterns rather than filled with the feeling and knowing of now. Character often pretends to speak truth but waters it down with qualifiers. Any indirect route takes us off course. When your character repeats history which is no longer true, you are held bound in that history.

A further step away from your true self is when you attribute power to outer circumstances. For example, you say that doing this activity for this long has made you tired. The external is given the power to tire you. The truth is, you have made yourself tired in relation to the circumstance. You have dissipated your attention, or ceased breathing consciously, or strayed into future worry, or . . .

## *Exercise:*

Close your eyes, stand tall, and ask yourself,

"Who am I in this moment and what qualities of character expression do I most often embody?"

Try speaking truth by breathing into self, registering what is there now in fresh acquaintance, and saying just that and nothing more.

Stand in the consciousness of yourself and identify the facts of Self. As you speak, listen through your feelings to see if what is being said is what you know. If the knowing is somewhat different, correct what you are saying and restate. You use your character as your vehicle of expression. What you know within you, give expression without.

Make notes of what you discovered.

Practice this throughout the day. Question any reporting of facts which do not feel true. Ask, is that really true?

## Scene Six
## *The Period of Creation: Emotional Experience*

Following the Period of Preparation is the **Period of Creation** in creating a life role.

The first way of creation is emotional experience: experiencing the feeling and letting it lead you to action. When you look at the action, you know what you were feeling. In contrast, to achieve an objective through the mind disenables one from living or experiencing what is played out. There is no functioning on the throughline.

I had a wonderful example of this in my life (one among many). My next door neighbors, an elderly Portuguese couple, lost their grown son to a stroke. They were both overcome with despair. The mother wailed with grief in her back yard and vowed to disown God for taking her son. She cried repeatedly, "Why me? Why him?" I knew there was little I could do to comfort her. I welled up with compassion and could not find a satisfactory way to express it, though I did reach out to her.

I stayed with the deep feeling of compassion for days, watching for what might emerge from it by way of action on my part. I "thought" of sending

## Act Six: I Am   277

flowers and other such offerings, but none of them seemed to sufficiently contribute to easing her loss. Then, from the midst of my deep feeling, there emerged an inner voice which told me to go immediately and write a book called *Why Me?* It was to be a handbook for the stricken. While I had written a few books before, I couldn't imagine writing one on this subject. I didn't think I knew enough about the subject, and especially what would become its subtitle, *How to Heal What's Hurting You.*

Because I was so decisively led from feeling to this action, I jumped right in. The flow of material from my inner knowing was powerful. In two and a half weeks the manuscript was completed and quickly sold to a publisher. I dedicated the book to my neighbors and have watched with gladness over the years as multiples of readers have benefited from *Why Me? How to Heal What's Hurting You.*

Consciousness work involves a courtship between Player and character. The emotional experience is the experience of union of the two, which makes creation possible.

### *Exercise to Music:*

If you can, invite a friend to participate with you. If not, use your imagination to create the partner as described below. If you have it, use the opening piece from the film, *The Mission*. If not, choose some other inspirational music.

One of you will represent character, the other, Player. Using movement only, allow a courtship to take place between Player and character. Begin with character courting Player. How does character call Player forth? How does character ask? How does character receive?

Then reverse. Player courts character. How? Where is the focus? Then make note of the differences you discovered.

The previous period of preparation with its four parts was a time of courtship between Player and character. This period of creation, in creating a life role, represents the consummation of the love between the two. The preparation was the conception and now we turn to the formation of the fruit of their union.

### *Exercise:*

Return to your partnership or your imaginative interaction. The courtship has taken place, back and forth, from character to Player and Player to character. Use the same music. Now, allow to evolve between you, organically, the consummation of the love between the two of you. Through movement, feeling, knowing, through an emotional experience that emerges from the midst of the two of you together in movement and feeling, let there be a union between the two and stay still in that union when you have come to it.

Then, if you are working with a partner, break out on your own into an experience of union of your own character with you, Player.

Do some written reflection: What is Union?

## Act Six: I Am 279

What most draws you into Union? What do you need to activate from Player to character to keep the connection consistent? What do you need to yield from character to Player?

Life is action. Life is a drama. Drama comes from the Greek word meaning *I do*. Action, though it appears externally, is first and truly internal, nonphysical, and a spiritual activity. As Stanislavski says, "It derives from an unbroken succession of independent processes; and each of these in turn is compounded of desires and impulses aimed at the accomplishment of some objective."[4] The movement is from Player to the character, from soul to body, from feelings to form.

> Sometimes an actor practically luxuriates in inaction, wallows in his own emotions. Blinded by the feeling that he is at home in his part, he thinks that he is creating something, that he is truly living the part. But no matter how sincere that passive feeling may be, it is not creative, and it cannot reach the heart of the spectator, so long as it lacks activity and does not promote the inner life of the play. When an actor feels his part passively his emotion remains inside him, there is no challenge to either inner or outer action.[5]

Even a passive state must be performed or

---
4 *Creating a Role,* page 49.
5 *Ibid.*

lived actively. Life, Stanislavski goes on, "is made up of continuously arising desires, aspirations, inner challenges to action and their consummation in internal and external actions."[6]

A life actor must "keep up a continuous fire of artistic desires all through his [life] part so that they in turn will arouse the corresponding inner aspirations, which then will engender corresponding inner challenges to act, and finally these inner calls to action will find their outlet in corresponding external, physical action."[7] The Will of the Larger is stirred as will in Player and that is, so to speak, incarnated as desires in the character, in your own nature, so that you become enmeshed with them. The desires must be embodied in actions and in physical body.

### *Exercise:*

Choose music for movement. A favorite of mine is *Planetary Unfolding,* by Michael Stearns. Close your eyes and follow urges and impulses while shaping the movement. Start up on your feet, free form. Then pull yourself into a ball on the floor and open up from there in slow motion and tiny increments.

Inner impulses are the motive power to outer action which is really spiritual activity. Before your response to circumstance, before there are objectives, there are the neurons of connection from

---

6 *Ibid.*
7 *Op. Cit.,* page 50.

Player to character. These are desires (unsatisfied), urges (from within), impulses that call for inner action and eventually for external action. These desires, urges, and impulses are motivating factors.

If you are feeling unmotivated it may be because you are dead to your emotional experience. Thus you are not creating anything. You are dead to the information that is coming, dead to desires, impulses, and urges.

Emotional experience results from feeling the urge and giving it life. Breathe down the throughline and bring the belly of your feeling into action. Don't go beyond the urge or shrink from it

## *Exercise:*

Put on instrumental music you haven't listened to in a while. Stand in the center of the room, listening and registering. Wait until the music moves you. Follow your impulses, allowing the inner to emerge so that you come to know it only as it manifests. Don't allow your mind to tell you what to do or how to move. This will give you a kinesthetic experience of how impulses motivate movement.

Next, jot down answers to the following:

> What is predominant in your emotional nature at this time of your life?
>
> What feelings are most prevalent?
>
> What actions are evoked by the feelings?
>
> What new feelings emerge from the actions?
>
> What do you communicate to your character through this?

## Scene Seven
# The Period of Creation: Creative Objectives

The second way of creation is through Creative Objectives.

Creative Objectives enable us to know the Will. The Will is the sustained impetus of Life-Force that sees an action through to completion. The action is what is needed to complete the objective.

Purpose derives from the Will, objective derives from purpose. From an objective you choose activities, which are what you do to achieve what you want, which take you into action.

Using my own life, here is an example of how purpose, creative objectives, activities, and actions might look. Note as I proceed that purpose, objectives and activities are always defined with active verbs. These stimulate energy to move. I will highlight the active verbs.

My life purpose is **to serve** the creative process.

My purpose in my work as a teacher and consciousness coach is **to guide** others in the process of embodying wisdom and fulfilling their potential.

My creative objectives are

**To communicate** the wisdom

**To articulate** clearly

**To model** the process of unfolding in consciousness

**To challenge** others to exceed their understanding

**To nurture** others as they do their inner work

**To grow** within myself as I encourage others to grow

How can I bring these objectives into reality and further my work purpose and therefore my life purpose? What do I do to achieve what I want? I identify strong activities to go with each creative objective.

*To communicate the wisdom:* Activities might be **to share, to speak boldly, to research and to develop** strong presentations

*To articulate clearly:* Activities might be **to carefully choose** words and concepts, **to provide** numerous examples, **to entice** with metaphors

*To model the process of unfolding in con-*

*sciousness:* Activities might be **to embody** whatever I suggest, **to demonstrate, to offer insights** in the moment they come

*To challenge others to exceed their understanding:* Activities might be **to direct** their efforts, **to gain** commitments, **to demand** that they demand more of themselves

*To nurture others as they do their inner work:* Activities might be **to inspire, to invite, to evoke, to praise, to encourage**

*To grow within myself as I encourage others to grow:* Activities might be **to shift** in their presence when I see something new, **to rephrase** as I hear myself speak, **to present** only current examples

Actions which might emerge from my creative objectives and activities might be:

*To communicate the wisdom:* **teach a class**

*To articulate clearly:* **write poetry using many images**

*To model the process of unfolding in consciousness:* **remain open to change in every moment**

*To challenge others to exceed their understanding:* **provide and direct exercises to give others practice**

*To nurture others as they do their inner*

***work:*** **create a non-judgmental learning environment**

***To grow within myself as I encourage others to grow:*** **reveal what needs changing and invite others to observe how I achieve that**

All purposes, objectives, activities, and actions are best fueled by feelings. Your feelings cannot be commanded or forced. They can only be coaxed as you yearn for action. The coaxing comes with your choices of creative objectives. These are motivating catalysts. Stanislavski tells us, "The objectives engender outbursts of desires for the purpose of creative aspiration. These desires send inner messages which naturally and logically are expressed in action. These objectives give a pulse to the living being..." of your character.[8]

The unfolding objectives are signals which, when seen altogether, show you your true direction. These objectives must be infused with life, with feeling, with zeal and enthusiasm. Stanislavski continues:

> If an actor achieves his objective purely through his mind he cannot live or experience his part, he can only give a report on it. Therefore he will not be a creator but a reporter of his role.
>
> The best creative objective is the unconscious [he is speaking of that which is

---
8  *Op. Cit.*, page 51.

not mentally produced but is organic] one which immediately, emotionally, takes possession of an actor's feelings, and carries him intuitively along to the basic goal of the play. The power of this type of objective lies in its immediacy (the Hindus call such objectives the highest kind of superconsciousness), which acts as a magnet to creative will and arouses irresistible aspirations. In such cases all the mind does is to note and evaluate the results . . . All we do is to learn how not to interfere with the creativeness of nature, or work to prepare the ground, seek out . . . means whereby even obliquely we can catch hold of these emotional, superconscious objectives.[9]

These objectives come into being intuitively as a result of the power of the emotional life and the exercise of the Will.

Objectives unfold organically, each one leading to the next. Feelings emerge that way as well. One and then another, and another — until the motive power is built into one grand impetus for creative activity. The unfolding is internal as well as external — feeling level as well as physical.

The unfolding is affected by interrelationship with others, by influences, by reactions, by how you are touched and stimulated. You extend from yourself forward, bringing your feelings into what you extend toward others. The interaction, first self-

---

9 *Op. Cit.,* page 52

with-self and then with self-with-another, follows a logical progression in which what is transpiring is revealed to you as you consciously participate.

You follow a progression of objectives which emerge as you emerge and as the interrelating emerges. You do not break from yourself or from the other and cling to feeling what you were feeling, waiting for the other to finish so that you can go on with what you were feeling. If you do this you break the inner line with yourself and with others. If you break the line you end up functioning more in unconscious patterns, in cliches, in conventional but empty ways.

Every life moment is a unit. Each unit has a minuscule objective. These begin to swarm like bees until the loud hum of what you are doing becomes heard by the whole of yourself. By cooperating, by bringing objectives into being, you listen and act, both making something happen and yielding to what is happening. The internal and external circumstances stir the Will and stir desire. These circumstances evoke creative aspirations, urged on by inner impulses to action. This is the process by which you put life into your life.

You stand in a point of delicate balance, listening to the drums of impulse beating within, heeding the intense emergent feeling, and giving voice and life to objectives through action. You yield and proceed. You stand firm and open into. This way of living needs to become habitual, needs to become second nature so that you can hear the voice of your soul and give it physical life in each moment.

### Exercise:

You might want to practice the above by engaging in an intimate sharing with another in which you tell that individual something about yourself that you have never told anyone (or only one other). Observe yourself as you speak to see if you put life into your life.

The more consciously you go forth into objectives, the greater will be your capacity to hear the inner promptings. This balance between inner and outer puts you at the point of singleness, the point of I, I AM. Stanislavski writes, "That is where human emotions exist in their pristine stage; there in the fiery furnace of human passions all that is trivial, shallow, is consumed, only the fundamental organic elements of an actor's creative nature remain."[10]

### Exercise:

Your purpose is **to sustain the will**. Your objective is **to know self intimately.** Achieve this purpose and objective by doing any of the following tasks:

1. Sit in stillness without moving for one hour
2. Walk in consciousness for one hour
3. Sit looking in a mirror focused on your own eyes for one hour
4. Swim in consciousness for one hour

---
10  *Op. Cit.,* page 77.

What enabled you to sustain the will to practice this discipline? What distracted you? What did you touch in yourself that can take you to a new level of consciousness and functioning?

## Scene Eight
## The Period of Creation: The Super-Objective

The third way of creation is The Super-Objective.

All objectives emerge from and converge in the innermost core of Self, in the I AM, in a Super-Objective. This Super-Objective is the all-embracing essence of all the life units. It cannot be known. It can only be uncovered in small bites. In it is contained the meaning for this life as aligned with the larger, unknowable meaning of all life.

Thinkers can conceptualize about life's grand meanings, about a Super-Objective, but it takes an artist, consciously committed to the art of life, to have an emotional experience of a Super-Objective — from which comes an aligning of character with Player. The Super-Objective becomes the main foundation of one's life. Living it fully, though it is unknown, becomes a pathway to the More that awaits you within. Moving from the inner to the outer, having an emotional experience of your creative action in the world, becomes a pathway to fulfilling more and more of your potential, of touching your potential greatness.

We cannot really say in limited words what the Super-Objective is. We can only continuously move closer to it. The closer we come the farther we are because the greater it has become in our advancing toward it. The journey in response to its allusiveness is artistic striving, which is the essence of creativity. In the striving we function on a throughline. Attainment of the Super-Objective is not actual but rather an unending urge which keeps us moving in the right direction.

All of this is completely different from how most of us live our lives. We are focused on achieving and therefore we gear ourselves toward tangible results. When we get those results we declare success. However, it is often true that success is lacking in meaning. We achieve but feel unsatisfied and move on to find fulfillment in something else where we agains seek results.

The wonderful thing about the unknowable Super-Objective is that it constantly urges us on and the urging, rather than results, is what feeds and nourishes us. The urging and the nourishment last a lifetime.

I had plans and aspirations for my life. I wanted to be a working actor in the theatre. I trained and even had a career for 18 years. But something else was cooking in my inner self about which I was totally unaware.

At age 19 I approached the secretary at my acting school about a mundane issue. Her head was bent down toward the desk so that I could not see her face. When Ev looked up, our eyes met and the room and everything that seemed to exist vanished. I can't tell you what I saw in her eyes, what held me transfixed. But instantly I was aware that she knew something I needed to know. So unformed was my awareness and the something I needed to know that I could not address what had just happened. I didn't know what to ask or what to say, but I knew something extraordinary had occurred. It was as if my life was divided in two, the part I had lived thus far and what the future had in store.

A year later Ev moved to Carmel, CA, and we began a newsy correspondence. Then, when I was 21, my first love Michael died. I was devastated. I wrote Ev and shared my grief. Her return letter spoke metaphorically about Michael travelling to the other side and being welcomed by those who loved him. I thought (mental level) that her words were very poetic, but they hit my inner self (spirit, intuition) with a jolt. Suddenly, although I didn't understand (mental level) what she was talking about, feelings began to roil in me and I was once again looking into Ev's eyes as she sat behind her desk two years before. I could feel something transforming in me but I had no idea what it was and therefore, once again, did not address it. The feelings were so strong they seemed to tell me that Ev not only knew something I needed to know but that I already knew what she knew. This was a powerful feel/know discovery.

Energy was moving in me; something unseen was urging me on. There was an unknown Super-Objective pushing me toward what I would now call

## Act Six: I Am   293

awakening. I could feel it but I couldn't identify it.

It was nine more years before I had any clarity, before I was ready to open to the More, to something totally new in my life. The awakening came following heart disease at age 29 and a trip across the country the next year when I stood face to face with Ev and our eyes locked as they had 11 years before. This time, I had already had an opening of the heart center (chakra) and I was ready for the cosmic awakening that occurred the next day on a trip down the Big Sur coastal highway in California when I looked into a flower and the whole of the energy world opened to me. I knew instantly that I was one with everything and there was no such thing as separation. What followed was a crash course in spiritual studies supplied by Ev, sleep instruction classes, receiving the six Love Principles, initiating The Love Project, etc., and a movement away from my original plans for my life and career.

While I still can't say what the Super-Objective is for my life, I can tell you that it pulls me forward into a blazing light that enables me to see the forces that bring manifestations into supposed reality.

As you continue your quest for the Super-Objective for your life, hold as an image for yourself these words written by Dancer Martha Graham to Agnes DeMille:

> There is a vitality, a life force, a quickening that is translated through you into action, and because there is only one of you in all time, this expression is unique.

> And if you block it, it will never exist through any other medium and be lost. The world will not have it. It is not your business to determine how good it is, nor how valuable it is, nor how it compares with other expressions. It is your business to keep it yours clearly and directly, to keep the channel open.
> You do not even have to believe in yourself or your work. You have to keep open and aware directly to the urges that motivate you.
> Keep the channel open...no artist is pleased...
> There is no satisfaction whatever at any time. There is only a queer, divine dissatisfaction; a blessed unrest that keeps us marching and makes us more alive than the others.[11]

Stanislavski tells us, "The Super-Objective and through-action are the inborn vital purpose and aspiration rooted in our being..."

I AM. Every life role has concealed within it a Super-Objective and a line of through-action. To step into consciousness of it is to have stepped onto a spiritual path, to have found a way to walk.

Stanislavski continues:

> The roots of the through-action are to be looked for in natural passions, in reli-

---
11 From the *Commonplace Book Collection.*

gious, social, political, aesthetic, mystical, and other feelings, in innate qualities or vices, in good or evil origins, whatever is most developed in the nature of man and which mysteriously governs him.[12]

Player desire is derived from the Super-Objective. This desire is stimulated by an urge which leads the character to strive. In each complete expression or action, there is an attainment. Player desire encounters conflict as it passes through the energy worlds from the unmanifested level to the manifested. Desire comes through the fires and is forged into actions. No action is carried out without obstacles. There are always counter movements, conflicting relationships, even self-limitations. These seeming outer conflicts are Player desire passing through the unseen barriers between worlds. They provide you with life drama which then enables you to look for the opportunity in what you think is a problem or crisis.

To cooperate with this ever ongoing process, as Player you must guide your character toward the constant fulfillment of the objectives you feel/know. This continuously activates the Will, minimizes doubt, and lights the way into the unknown that is unfolding only as you step closer to what is calling.

The superconscious or intuitive is available to the feeling level, not to the mind. Polished techniques cannot take you there. According to Stanislavski:

---

[12] *Op. Cit.,* page 79

The more subtle the feeling, the closer it comes to the superconscious, the closer to nature, and the farther is it removed from the conscious. The superconscious begins where reality, or rather the ultra-natural, ends, where nature becomes exempt from the tutelage of the mind, exempt from conventions, prejudices, force. Thus the natural approach to the superconscious is through the unconscious. The only approach to the superconscious, to the unreal, is through the real, the ultra-natural, that is to say through nature and its normal, unforced, creative life.[13]

Your work, then, is not to seek to control or even to plan, but to prepare, to constantly open yourself and make ready by listening and taking the small actions necessary to manifest what is emerging from within. This is the purpose for having a character self through which to function. It is the outer creation of what you register.

### *Exercise:*

Once again choose instrumental music.

Stretch your character by giving it a series of qualities to embody while walking to the music. For example, determined, lazy, hesitant.

Move in these qualities to the music, discover-

---

13 *Op. Cit.,* page 82.

ing feelings and urges and giving them life. Formulate an objective for each quality and move it purposefully into action. What do you tell yourself about yourself through this choice of objective and action?

Next, embody these qualities to music: classy, sensual, greedy. Again make discoveries as above. Formulate an objective for each quality and move it purposefully into action. What do you tell yourself about yourself through this choice of objective and action?

Does this stretching of character lead you along the path of gaining an inkling of your Super-Objective?

Write a clear, honed statement of a major objective by which you currently live your life in order to respond to your larger purpose. Use the most powerfully descriptive words you can.

## Scene Nine
# The Period of Creation: Physical Embodiment

The fourth way of creation is through Physical Embodiment (of the self you are, the character you already portray on the stage of life).

You might want to try this with a friend. If not, do it by yourself, for yourself.

### Exercise:
Stand in front of your friend and read your honed statement of a major objective by which you live. Then give the paper to your friend and hear it read to you. Compare the strength of delivery.

Then, ask your friend to read it again. This time give the objective life in your physical body. Give it sound, walk in it, move in it, let it lead you into unplanned movements and actions. Discover it and yourself in it. Let feelings emerge, expand into, through and with the objective.

Then, read it again. Tell your friend how it applies to your life right now, as in changes you need to make in current action.

## Act Six: I Am

You will now proceed to physical embodiment of facets of yourself that wait to emerge. They push from the inside out, from the core of I AM into embodiment in new form. It is as if it is a "new" character, birthed in the moment as you focus on being true to urges, impulses, desires, feelings.

What emerges will be new on many levels. There will be the verbal level: sounds, words, phrases, perhaps sentences and even on to statements depending on the degree of development as you proceed and as you listen within before uttering. Within every word there is an inner something that justifies its very being. If not, it should not be spoken.

Stanislavski spoke of this in these words:

> Empty words are like nutshells without meat, concepts without content; they are of no use, indeed they are harmful. They weigh down a [life] role, blur its design; they must be thrown out like so much trash.[14]

The conscious state may be described, in part, as one in which there are no superfluous moments, or feelings, or words, or movements. Anything less is a state of awareness ,though we often rush to label it conscious. Further, it is not enough to think something, expound something, or even to know

---
14 *Op. Cit.,* page 94.

something. Aligning ourselves with our current life circumstances and the growing edge therein, we need to convert what we know into living terms. We need to embody it.

I began attending Broadway plays in 1953 during my first year at the High School of Performing Arts. In that year I saw "Tea and Sympathy" and it left a lasting imprint on my consciousness because of a single gesture at the end of the play. It was a perfect example of the power of physical embodiment. Laura (Deborah Kerr), the wife of a coach at a prep school, becomes a caring, loving influence in the life of a sensitive student, Tom, played by John Kerr. The boy is confused about his sexuality and her objective is to help him into manhood. She does this at the end by offering herself in an intimate scene.

I was sitting in the last row of the balcony but it was as if I was right there with them in their tender quiet moment. Her last line is, "Years from now when you talk about this, and you will, be kind." Her objective was played out in a single action, lasting only a few seconds as the curtain fell. She leaned over him, saying her line, and she slowly began to open the buttons on her blouse. So simple a physical movement and yet so powerful that it has lasted in my consciousness well over half a century. This is what is meant by nothing superfluous, nothing excess. This was filling the words with full life.

Here is an opportunity for you to practice physical embodiment.

## *Exercise:*

Begin by describing in your journal a scene from your life that represents conflict between you and another or between you and an event or an aspect of your life. Make notes of qualities that were most alive in you at the time.

Next, speak out loud about it, this time speaking in third person, as if it were real. If it were real, what would you be doing or feeling? How would you physically move and express if you were in a scene like this? Give it life.

Then, speak in first person, using "I." Enter the sharing of the conflict as if for the first time with fresh impressions and a reappraisal of the facts. As you speak, see your character anew in this situation with all the new possibilities.

Make notes of your discoveries.

Later, in words and images and metaphors, use your creative imagination to describe your ideal character exactly as you would like it to be in form and expression. You have the benefit of all you have been and have learned, and you can now embellish this character with no restrictions, except for this: make the description true to your urges, desires, and current capabilities. Save these notes as you will use them a bit later.

## Scene Ten
## *The Period of Creation: Physical Embodiment*
### *(Continued)*

Physical action is the illustration of the experience you have within. That inner experience calls to you. Intuition is converted into fact by embodied action. Every move, every muscle is a vehicle of conveyance of the inner self. This, as a truth, is thwarted by your haphazard use of your body. Every physical movement and expression should be fully and directly subordinated to feeling. You are the dancer of your inner process.

Tension, excess, and involuntary movements distort your own knowledge of yourself and your communication to others. Be in charge of what goes forth as expression.

Stanislavski says it clearly:

> Let the body go into action when it can no longer be held back, when it feels the deep inner essence of experienced emotions, inner objective which it has prompted. Then of its own volition there will emerge an instinctive, natural urge to carry out the

## Act Six: I Am

aspirations of creative will in the form of physical action . . . nothing is accomplished by prohibitions.[15]

He says that prohibitions merely create excess tension.

It is a kind of law that cliché will fill any empty space much as weeds will do out of doors. A gesture which is made for its own sake is a piece of force perpetrated on one's inner feelings and their natural manifestation. . . Alas for the actor if there is a slippage between his body and his soul, between his inner action and his outward movements. Alas for him if his bodily instrument falsifies his feelings, puts them off the right key. It is what happens to a melody played on an instrument out of tune. And the truer the feeling, the more painful the discordance. . . The shape must conform to the inner substance. . . The ability to keep one's body completely at the service of one's feelings is a principal concern of the external technique of incarnating a role.[16]

All this that Stanislavski says about the actor absolutely applies to you in your creation of a life role. All the bits and pieces of the creative process fit together like a puzzle, enabling you to come clos-

15  *Op. Cit.,* page 102.
16  *Op. Cit.,* page 103.

er to knowing the Super-Objective.

I urge you to rent and watch the film *The Hiding Place*. As the film progresses, watch for the Super-Objective in the characters in the film. While you know it is unknowable, look for how it is embodied in the life purposes of characters. How are they true to their purposes and objectives on the throughline? How do they guide their characters to embody their values?

What was the life purpose of each of the major characters, revealing something of the Super-Objective? What specific objectives did they play? What activities aided them? How did they embody their inner knowing?

Where do you waiver in your faith and how can you strengthen that link?

## *Exercise:*

Reflect on how you experienced yourself when you began to consciously look at who you knew yourself to be. What were your predominant characteristics and ways of being? What was your tempo and rhythm? Walk around in this now, move in it, and make the sound of it.

Now reflect on how you get in the way of expressing your highest and best. As answers come to you, fully embody the distracting characteristics, physical life, the tempo and rhythm. Give life to your character in an unconscious state.

Next, review your description of the Ideal character you would like to create.

## Act Six: I Am

Now give yourself a fun test. Choose three different characteristics or bundles of characteristics you want to bring to life in your ideal character. Then, get in your car and drive to a shopping mall.

Choose one quality or bundle of characteristics and breath it in. Then go to a clothing store. Embody the quality or qualities as you try on garments that speak to you of this quality or bundle, consciously becoming what you are creating, thread by thread. Activate the observer facet of yourself during the dressing. Observe the characteristics, the behavior, the choices you make of store, of garments, etc. Observe the feelings, urges, impulses and follow-through. Observe what responses come to you from clerks as you embody these qualities.

Following the experience write a full report of your discoveries about yourself.

Then go to a second store. Embody another characteristic or bundle. Follow the same procedure and record differences and discoveries.

And then, repeat this in a third store. Make notes of all your discoveries.

Spend time reflecting on what is no longer true of you at all. What ways of functioning have you released?

What are you in process with but still stands in the way of your functioning at your highest and best?

What is new for you that you want to develop?

What can you as Player do to develop these qualities and ways of functioning?

## Scene Eleven
# The Period of Creation: Physical Embodiment
### (Continued)

When you consciously move your body, and especially when you make specific gestures for emphasis, it is important that feelings and sensory awareness fill each of those movements. The result is a marriage of your consciousness and your body, your inner spirit and your intention.

If you have organic physical truth in a given action, your feelings will respond to your inner faith in the genuineness of what your body is doing. This enables you to commune with yourself so that your soul opens to receive the Super-Objective.

Every action takes you forward into the More waiting to be discovered. Don't distract yourself with mind worry. Enact with objectives that enable you to initiate. Always ask *what next* rather than *what if*.

It is so important in so many areas of your life to ask *what* rather than *if*. I think of airline pilots in life and death situations who focus only on landing, never doubting, not focusing at all on the possibility of not landing. Their attention is on *what* — what do I need to do now?

A clear way for character to align with Player intention is to have faith in your physical actions (given that they are fully expressed, and that you allow them to take you forward into the new that is waiting to be manifested). This opens the door to feeling your emotional life, or in other words, to knowing through external life the internal life of Player. A bond is formed from outer to inner, from inner to outer.

Physical actions evoke feelings which lead to knowing because there is an unbreakable bond between the action and what precipitated it. You do not come to understand as much as know this union between the spiritual and the physical. And the knowing originates in the feelings. You don't think/comprehend, you feel/know.

You are now ready for the major project of Act Six.

## *Exercise:*

There are several things you will need for this. You will need a partner, rehearsal time, several friends, and a space to convene everyone.

Before you begin, once again read your statement of the ideal character you wish to create. Rework it if you need to. Remember that this should be a description of a character that you can fully embody right now. Add in everything you want to

## Act Six: I Am

birth in and through yourself. Choose only those things that you can actually begin to do right now. Then add five things you know you are almost ready to embody but don't quite know how to do it or sustain it. Have this information fresh in your consciousness.

Because it is sometimes difficult to get your own character to change and become what you want (because you are too close to it, or because its habits are too ingrained), I give you the opportunity to have a "loaner character" with which to work, a clone of your character.

You will select a partner, same-sex is easiest, to be your loaner. With the help of this partner, you will commence to incarnate a character, to birth a representation of self that is in alignment with the inner. To embody the new you will focus on fresh acquaintance. As you "give birth," listen to everything and be open to each unfolding moment. Ward off preconceptions. Be organic. Allow yourself to discover what is true, what is enough but not excessive, what is vital to what is calling, and what is fundamental to the creation.

This is the beginning of birthing a character, a character through which to function in the world, one that is aligned with you as Player. The character should be eager for your observations, and receptive to and compliant with your directions. It should serve you in all ways and be an expression of your creative nature so that you can embody who you are in your finest frequency and make that visible in the world.

As you proceed with the creation of this character, choose only those characteristics that fulfill this task. You will practice by directing the loaner character to embody these. The loaner character will have the task of stripping from him/herself qualities which make it identifiable. The loaner character, wearing a solid color — all black, or all blue, or all white — will embody only what you direct.

Using this loaner, create the ideal character, in every way, for your fine frequency functioning. Everything should be aligned: the physical movement, the rhythm, the tempo, the speech, the voice, the behavior, the interaction with others, the purposes and objectives, the way you listen, the way you see, the thoughts you allow in your private world, etc. Take the time to train this loaner. You may take it out into the community to interact with others while you give it feedback on how to become your highest and best expression.

As you rehearse with your clone, be open to a fresh impression of your basic character. What are you learning about directing character? What new techniques can you employ with your own character? Ask your clone what he/she has learned about how to serve you better when functioning as your character? This will be very helpful information for you.

## Scene Twelve
## *The Period of Creation: Physical Embodiment*
### *(Continued)*

Once you have had sufficient time working with and developing the clone into your perfect character representation, invite a group of friends over to a space large enough for all of you to be able to move about if necessary.

In preparation for the time with them, design an experience in which they will participate. It could be a growth experience, a fun learning experience, or even a game. Whatever you choose, your ideal character (your clone) will conduct the experience while you (Player) will actively direct the ideal character (the clone), making sure that each and every thing it does, word it says, movement it makes, is precisely what you want to bring into being as the ideal character through which you will live your life.

### *Exercise:*
When everyone is gathered, begin by reading to your friends your statement of the ideal charac-

ter self you would like to create. Tell them to watch for these qualities and also to be aware of the impact of those qualities on them. What do they feel and experience?

You are ready now to apply all of the above in a live experience.

Give the loaner character an assignment to relate to those gathered utilizing the specific experience that you devised. As the loaner interacts with them, you direct, refine, and demonstrate, in everyone's presence, until the loaner character is a harmonious expression of what you are seeking. During this time with your friends, you will be dressed in the attire that calls forth the "perfect" character through which you want to function.

Now comes the most important step. When the loaner achieves what you are looking for, you will take over. The clone will join the group and you will step into what you have just created and you will become the ideal expression of you as Player. You will continue to interact with those present in the experience you have devised and everyone will relate to you in return.

Following the experience, the loaner (your clone) will report on what it was like to be trained and to perform. You will then report on yourself. Your friends will then give you feedback.

Your ability to embody and sustain your choice of a "visible self" will be your measure of what you have learned and digested during six acts of **The Theatre of Life.** In this project, you will have birthed an aligned self through which to live consciously in the world.

## Scene Thirteen
## *Conscious Embodiment*

Your use of consciousness in acting through a character is your responsibility. Your character is dependent on you for its life. If you are not fully "in" the character you have created in the world, your character will be deprived of live feelings and cannot in turn come to experience union with you.

In order for you to come out on the stage of life as a human being you must always know who you are, what has just happened to you, under what circumstances you are functioning here, where you have come from (in inner self), why you are here, and how you are being here now. Just to walk in the world you need always to sense life being lived around you and your relation to it.

Every inner and outer action of yours must be truthful. You must always have a purpose and objectives. And these should be prompted by inner impulses.

If you are not living fully through your character, being passionately present to feelings, desires, impulses, and urges, you are living only in the mind of your character. Understanding is once removed from knowing. In fully creating the physical life, you are recreating the spiritual life which is stimulating your actions. The more you pay attention to what you bring into being, the more you will come to know what is guiding you on the spiritual plane, and the closer you will come to the Super-Objective. All of this will lead you to inner union, a state devoutly to be wished for.

## Scene Fourteen
## *Direct Registry of Frequencies*

Begin every engaging with life circumstances in which you 'find yourself' with these questions: What would I do if I were in this situation? and What is essential to fill my objective?

I can't tell you how important this is. If you identify with your character/personality self and think that what is happening in the situation is happening to *you*, you are caught in that situation because you are identified with the character to whom it appears to be happening. You are not that character; you are Player and you have creative jurisdiction over that character. Therefore, you can ask yourself (as Player): What would I do if this actually happened to my character? How would I want to respond? What resources can I bring to the moment? What objectives would most serve me? What reality do I want to create? If you are identified with character you cannot ask any of these questions. You do not have creative jurisdiction. You do not have any power. You cannot direct yourself if you slip into lesser functioning. You cannot bring yourself back to the path that is harmonious for you.

One of my great life examples of this came in March, 2010, when I was diagnosed with breast cancer. I did not identify with the cancer or with the character who had the cancer. I immediately reminded myself that I was Player and that I had creative jurisdiction over how I would respond, how I would care for character, and how I would deal with the cancer. First and foremost was to create a sense of peace and calm in which there was no fear or worry. From there I was free to make decisions for the body's well-being. I could lead my character through the whole process of surgery and recovery because I continued to ask myself: *what would I do if I were in this situation and what is essential to fill my objective?*

When you are out there in your character self, performing physical actions and functioning in relation to a whole dynamic to which you have turned your attention, make conscious choices about what you say and how you say it. Infuse your expressions with feeling, with vivid life expression. Listen to the others who speak to you and receive what they say through an open heart chakra. Focus on feeling, seeing, hearing, giving, and merging. Let your energy and physical body be alive and fluid. Feel the pulsing of the life force moving through you as you bring your whole self to the exchange. That life force is the Living Spirit and if you yield to it you will move beyond the illusion of separation.

Activate your intuition, your imagination, and your inner self and you will sense your soul alive and vibrant. You will catch a shining glimmer of the state of "I Am."

## *Exercise:*

For a final exercise you might want to play the opening music from the movie *Chariots of Fire* and symbolically walk from the memory of who you used to be, into the light beyond the apron on the stage of life. Allow yourself to be pulled into the future of all that you can become. Feel the fire of the past at your back and the unlimited power that is yours now and in the future pulling you forward.

You have traversed six Acts of **The Theatre of Life.** You are at the beginning and ready to live in consciousness, exercising creative jurisdiction over all you do and all you are.

## Sources of Inspiration and Training for the Creation of
## The Theatre of Life

The main contributing factor to the birth of **The Theatre of Life** was my breakthrough to Cosmic Consciousness in 1969 which enabled me to know who I really am as a Being. That awakening opened the floodgates of my potential, allowed me to see profoundly with my inner eye, and greatly enhanced my already-developed intuition. It encouraged me to reclaim and restructure a wealth of learning and training from earlier years and to bring forth new forms that would serve others in their unfolding process.

I retrieved knowledge that grew out of the human potentials movement. I had been particularly moved by the perspective of Humanistic Psychologist Abraham Maslow (*Toward a Psychology of Being,* NY: Van Nostrand), most especially his focus on becoming the more of who we are rather than being mired in healing the lesser with which we too often identify.

I also resurrected my years of training as an actor and director. In the world of theatre, the teachings of Constantin Stanislavski (often referred to as "The Method") were the foundation of my acting career.

Maslow and Stanislavski both encouraged a form of reaching for the stars and beyond. I remember being told during my acting training that Stanislavski never wanted to publish his techniques because he wanted his students to go beyond what he had developed. Inspired by his work, I hope I have added a small innovative step to his great contribution.

Stanislavski's techniques have been taught for years by many theatre giants. I learned many variations of those techniques during my years in the Drama Department of The High School of Performing Arts in New York City and at the HB Studio in New York during four years of acting technique study with Irene Dailey and two years of scene study with Uta Hagen. I applied all that teaching to my experience as a professional actor.

In 1981, nine years after retiring from acting and directing, leaving New York City, and nine years after beginning my work with Diane Kennedy Pike, disseminating **The Love Principles** in experiential "Practice Sessions" that encouraged participants to function consciously and embody unconditional love, the world of theatre called to me once again. I returned to Stanislavski's books and saw in a whole new light, through the eyes of an awakened being, what he had created for his actors. What he taught actors, I realized, could be used to teach "ordinary" human beings to grab the reins of their creativity and bring their own lives to fruition, consciously!

Prior to awakening I had studied many books on the Ancient Wisdom, including The Alice Bailey Series, Lucis Publishing Company; *The Kingdom of the Gods* by Geoffrey Hodson; *Breakthrough to Creativity by* Shafica Karagulla; *The Unobstructed Universe* by Stewart Edward White; three books by Vera Stanley Alder, including *The Finding of the Third Eye, Initiation of the World,* and *The Fifth Dimension*; and works by Corinne and Theodore Heline.

I had also experienced training during my sleep in "classes" conducted in the Energy World. I was able to bring this teaching into manifestation when I committed to becoming what I had learned. Once I started to do that, my life became an ongoing "practice session" in being a living example of what I knew.

Thus, in 1981, I began a six-year process of combining my theatrical experience and training with the Wisdom teachings so that I could create **The Theatre of Life** for those who wanted to consciously create the role they were living, to fulfill their potential, and to exercise creative jurisdiction over their lives.

*Stanislavski Works Cited:*

Stanislavski, Constantin, *An Actor Prepares*, New York: Theatre Arts Books: Robert M. MacGregor, 1956

_____, *Building a Charactor,* New York: Theatre Arts Books: Robert M. MacGregor, 1949

_____, *Creating a Role,* New York: Theatre Arts Books, 1961

## About the Author

**Arleen Lorrance** created **The Theatre of Life** in 1981 and served as its Artistic Director for the next 26 years. She graduated from the High School of Performing Arts in New York, earned a B.A. from Brooklyn College and an M.F.A. in Stage Direction from the City University of New York. She was a professional actor, a director of Drama Programs throughout New York City, and served as Chairperson of the Speech and Theatre Department at a Brooklyn high school where she introduced **The Love Project** and the six **Love Principles.**

Arleen has published numerous books on consciousness work, plus a book of poetry and a novel. She is a Personal Consciousness Coach, has taught classes on the Ancient Wisdom, and has conducted countless workshops with her partner Diane Kennedy Pike for over 40 years. See www.consciousnesswork.com for more information.

Arleen resides in Scottsdale, Arizona, and enjoys bringing her many skills to groups and individuals across the continent. She may be contacted at angeloso@aol.com.

www.ingramcontent.com/pod-product-compliance
Lightning Source LLC
Chambersburg PA
CBHW031231290426
44109CB00012B/249